Baby Animals
[1001] photos

[1O01] photos

Baby Animals

© 2006 Éditions Solar, an imprint of Place des Éditeurs
© 2007 Rebo International, b.v., Lisse, The Netherlands

This edition printed in 2009.

Text: Corinne Francois Huart and Ségolene Roy
Photography: Yves Lanceau and furrytails.nl
Coordination: Isabelle Raimond
Graphic design: Gwénaël Le Cossec
Translation: First Edition Translations Ltd, Cambridge, UK
Typesetting: A.R. Garamond, Prague, Czech Republic

ISBN: 978 90 366 2255 4

Baby Animals
[1001]
[photos]

REBO
PUBLISHERS

Table of Contents

Birth

First steps

Training and games

Family life

Everyday life

In a town, on a farm

Birth

Laying eggs is a common feature of most fish, amphibians and birds as well as insects. Having carried out this task, some parents simply disappear into the blue and leave their offspring at the mercy of Mother Nature whereas others build nests, look after their eggs and care for their young.

In most cases, the egg develops outside its mother's body, however, some reptiles, such as blindworms or adders and some shark species, carry their eggs inside their bodies before they have fully developed. Their young are then live born and do not have to struggle to hatch. Eggs come in different shapes and colors, while the conditions they are laid in are as varied as the world around them. Fish and frogs eggs mature in water and they are, quite logically, soft and jelly-like. Fish spawn, once abandoned by their parents, must seek food immediately after they hatch in order to survive. They feed on plants and algae, on which they are also often born.

Reptile eggs have a shell which ensures they do not dry out; mollusc eggs are round and glossy, and are often buried in the ground where the embryos develop.

Many terrestrial animals do, nevertheless, lay their eggs in water; their larvae remain there until they are fully developed and are ready to undergo metamorphosis. The Dung (scarab) beetle lays its numerous eggs in cowpats and dung which consequently serves as nutrition for the larvae. Butterflies lay eggs on plants which then serve as food for their larvae. It provides them with all the necessary nutrients.

Hard limy shells are typical for bird eggs. Most lay their eggs in nests. When the Booby bird covers its eggs it hides them underneath its body and protects them with its legs. The Emperor penguin, on the other hand, keeps its single egg in a special pouch made of skin. This protects the egg against

Leaving the egg

low temperatures. This is done because some embryos need plenty of warmth in order to hatch. The eggs of the marine turtle are hidden in sand while the eggs of some snake species can be found under fallen and decaying leaves. The crocodile is one of the few reptiles that maintains interest after the birth of its babies.

Shortly after mating, the female starts building its nest. With its hind legs, it digs a hole in the sand some 24 inches in diameter and lays fifteen to eighty eggs into it, which she then covers to keep them warm. Some reptile species, such as the Mississippi alligator, prefer a shaded place near water. The reptile collects twigs, fallen branches and soil and only then buries its egg into this "nest." Decomposing plants produce the vitally important heat. The incubation temperature in fact determines the gender of the young reptile. The mother guards the nest from nearby and if necessary fiercely protects its eggs against any daring predators. It can survive without food for the three month incubation period. By making small cries and growls, the embryo informs the mother that it is about to break out of the egg. She then finds her nest and digs out the egg. When the shell breaks, the female reptile takes its young one in its mouth and transports it into the water. For several days the young remain close to their mother, either on her back or on her head. If

they happen to stray, they call the adults with abrupt squeals, and are immediately returned to the safety of the group. At this stage of their life, they are also helpless and very vulnerable. There are eagles, carnivorous fish and mongooses out there, on the lookout for these infants. They are not completely safe even from the males of their own kind as cannibalism is not unknown. At the end of this short period, the family breaks up.

[1] A newborn Nile crocodile with a caruncle, a tiny horn-shaped pike at the end of its muzzle.
[2] Immediately after a young crocodile hatches out of its egg, its mother takes it gently in its mouth and transports its little baby into the water.

[3] A Nile crocodile needs several hours of hard work to get out of its hard-shelled egg.
[4] Newborn crocodiles are approximately 12 inches long.
[5] If an egg is too hard to break, the mother cracks it open by rolling the egg between its tongue and palate.
[6] Since baby crocodiles are easy prey for eagles and mongooses, they stay close to their protective mother at all times.

[1-2] Green and yellow grass snakes lay 5-15 eggs. Six to eight weeks later, snakes of 8–10 inches in length hatch with bodies covered in yellow, grey and brown dots.

[3] The bite of the African house snake is completely harmless. Even though the bite of an adult snake can be rather painful, the bite of a baby snake will only result in a minor flesh wound.

[4] The chameleon lays its eggs into a nest directly in the ground.
[5] Honduran milk snakes (*lampropeltis hondurensis*), very often eat siblings from the same nest.
[6] The corn snake (or red rat snake) can grow up to six and a half feet in length.

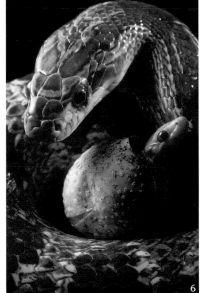

[1-2] An ostrich lays up to 12 eggs. A young ostrich hatches after around 42 days and it sometimes needs up to 50 hours to get out of its egg.

1 **2**

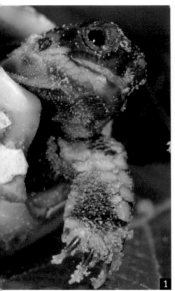

3 [1-3] The Hermann Tortoise is the only terrestrial tortoise native to France. It is a highly endangered species and can nowadays only be found in a small area in the Var region and in Corsica. In spring, the female lays approximately ten eggs in a sunny and warm place. The baby tortoises hatch in late summer. [2] The Greek (or Moorish) tortoise lays 3–12 eggs with an incubation period of 60–90 days.

4

5

[4] The purple heron builds its nest amongst the reeds on lake shores and in glades.
[5] The brown noddy nests on tropical or subtropical islands.
[6] The herring gull is a very social animal which prefers to build its nest among large colonies.
[7] The Patagonian goose lays its eggs in a nest made of down and feathers.

6

7

[1-3] The Rockhopper penguin (1) and the King penguin (3) keep their single egg warm hidden in the belly in a special pouch.
[2] The Eurasian curlew breeds in an area that stretches from Western Europe to the Arctic Circle.
[4] The southern giant petrel lays its eggs in late August and its fledglings hatch in late October.
[opposite page] The eggs of the moorhen in a floating nest.

An impregnated mammal's egg grows and develops in the womb in the form of an embryo which leaves the mother's uterus as a fully developed and relatively robust creature in comparison with an egg. Even though the newborn is weak and exposed, it has nevertheless reached the stage when it is more or less capable of surviving.

Apart from marsupials, whose young are born at the embryonic stage, all other mammals, from mice to elephants, give birth to fully developed infants. They are also referred to as "viviparous animals," meaning that mothers give birth to living offspring. Smaller species, such as rabbits, dogs and cats, usually have more than one baby. A female hedgehog, for example, gives birth to a litter of five or more young and an opossum can have as many as twelve infants in a litter. Pandas, elephants and monkeys, on the other hand, usually only have a single baby.

The gestation period also differs substantially among various species: one month in rabbits, five months in goats, twelve months in zebras and twenty two long months in elephants. Once this period, vitally important for the growth and development of the embryo, is over, a newborn infant gets its first chance to draw breath outside of its mother's uterus.

Carnivorous animals have a tendency to make the birth somewhat easier and less strenuous by lying down, whereas herbivorous animals stand on all four legs whilst giving birth. This is also the case with giraffes, tall as they are. Sea mammals, if they are able, return to land to give birth because in the very beginning their young ones would not survive in water.

Bats and tree sloths give birth upside-down, the baby then slipping down the mother's stomach. The first instinct of the mother, where necessary, is to sever the umbilical cord, to clean and rid its

Leaving the womb

baby of any remaining amniotic fluid and blood with its tongue and finally to dry and warm the little animal up. In this way, a baby and its mother learn to recognise and identify each other by their scent because for many female mammals the idea of taking care of another's baby is absolutely unacceptable.

[1] When born, the infant of the Red colobus monkey is completely white from head to toe. Its hair only darkens after several months of life.
[2] After 330 days of gestation, the female addax antelope gives birth to a single baby.
[3] The Thompson gazelle gives birth to a litter of one or two calves after 165 days of pregnancy.

[4-5] A litter of four to five little hedgehogs is born after a month of gestation. The female will nurse them over a period of three weeks.
[6] Lion cubs are born after three and a half months of gestation and will consequently be nursed for two and a half months.

[1] A baby aurochs (European bison) is born after a gestation of nine months.

[2] The European bison calf will be fully grown after around 6 years when its weight reaches approximately 1500 pounds.

[3] A calf learns to recognize its mother by her scent. Most female mammals will only take care of their own offspring.

Birth

[4] The common otter reproduces throughout the whole year; the mating itself takes place in water. After 60 days the female gives birth to 1, 2 or 3 tiny baby otters.
[5-6] The gestation period of mice is 21 days and there are 5-12 tiny mice in a litter.
[7] When a female chamois gives birth, the new-born are watched by all the members of the herd.

4

5

6

7

[1] A Galapagos sea lion cub, a species which is on the list of endangered species. Thanks to the protection laws, this baby can peacefully spend endless hours lying on the beach with its mother.
[2] The southern elephant seal is born on sandy beaches. As an adult it will reach an impressive weight of 3 tons; a female will weigh more then 1700 pounds.

[1 – 7] After mating, the mare gives birth to a foal after 11 months of gestation. In this picture, the birth is taking place under the close supervision of a veterinarian. The birth itself is very quick and does not take longer then quarter of an hour. The mare then licks its foal and nudges it with its muzzle to help it stand up. Immediately afterwards, the foal, standing on all four legs, begins hungrily to suckle from its mother.

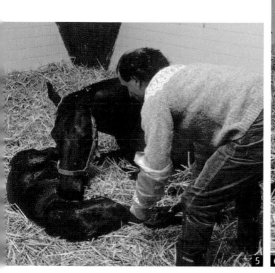

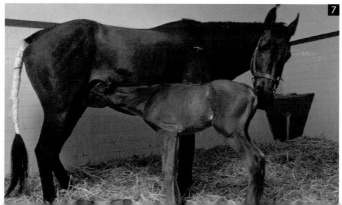

[1] A fawn, initially covered in white and yellow spots, grows into a buck in one year.
[2] The Bontebok antelope is native to South Africa and Lesotho. Due to unrestricted hunting, its numbers have massively declined and nowadays it survives mainly thanks to controlled reproduction in nature reserves and zoos.

Many mammals, such as cows, elephants and giraffes, give birth in the open air and to do so, they choose more or less protected places. These species do not feel any need to provide their young ones with shelter. They are referred to as precocial animals, mature and mobile upon birth, and therefore not needing protection. Other animals, altricials, are not at all capable of surviving independently after entering the world.

A hole or a den is therefore an absolute necessity for them. They do not yet have a coat of hair or fur, they are delicate and vulnerable and their mothers therefore keep them warm in their lairs. Some parents are very gifted builders. When they feel the moment of birth is approaching, these animals start searching for a secure and sheltered place where they set up a temporary home for their young. While some birds build rather

Born in a hole, born in a den

When a fox is about to give birth to cubs it sometimes digs out a den, but more often chooses to settle in another's den (for example a badger's set). A fox gives birth to 3–5 cubs, sometimes more.

complex nests, most mammals are not precise enough for such a delicate task. More often than not, they make do with a hole in the ground or with a hollow in a tree or amongst rocks. A lynx will usually give birth in a small cave or in a recess in rocks whereas a jaguar gives birth in the open space of the savannah.

Some are true animal architects though. A squirrel will build a nest out of leaves, moss and fragments of honeysuckle bark. Usually it places its nest on branches where, if built properly, it can remain intact for many years, despite unfavourable weather conditions.

A badger's burrow is a true maze made of a number of rooms of different sizes and shapes. They are kept clean and tidy, straw and grass-lined, and are equipped with a shaft for the disposal of excrement. The polar bear will, on the other hand, dig a cave not dissimilar to an igloo. The entrance is sealed off by a mass of snow and thanks to the heat of the mother's body the ambient temperature inside may reach 50 to 68 °F, far higher than the outside temperature.

[1-2] Laughing hyena cubs are born in dens which are also being used by other members of the pack; hyenas only set out on their hunting expeditions after sunset.

[3-4] These helpless wild rabbit kittens are only one week old and have just crawled out of their den for the very first time.
[5] A one month old rabbit on a daring journey into the furthest reaches of its den.
[6-7] Stone martens mate twice a year, in July and August and then in February and March. Newborn animals weigh approximately one ounce.

35

[1-2] The central part of the den, where the coyote pups are born, is some 6 and a half feet long and is usually located around 3 feet underground. Coyotes also dig their dens under big hollow tree trunks, in widened rock cavities or they will even make do with an abandoned human dwelling.
[3] An arctic fox cub emerging from its den in the spring, its fur brown. As winter approaches, it turns white.

[4] In the wild, hamster pups are born in small dens. In captivity, females give birth in a nest made of cotton wool and covered with straw.
[5-6] Meerkats are burrowing animals and always give birth near their den. Most of the time they are on the alert, standing up straight on the look out for predators.

[1] The female harvest mouse is capable of building a completely enclosed nest within 48 hours. There, it usually gives birth to 3–8 baby mice.
[2] Garden dormice are born and hibernate in nests made of straw.

[1-2-4-5-6] The female American black bear spends the winter in a den where she also gives birth to her bear cubs. The family leaves its shelter in April or May. The young ones stay with their mother for a whole year and then begin to live independently. [3] The Grizzly bear also belongs to the family of American bears. A hump on the back of its head is the main distinguishing feature. Grizzly bear cubs weigh approximately one pound. As adult animals, they will weigh more than half a tonne.

41

Penguins, as well as some other bird species, do not build nests for their young. Some birds, on the other hand, will construct the most intricate and durable nest structures, especially if the baby is to spend most of its initial growth period in the nest. They are mostly made of feathers, wool and hair, and are hidden within trees, in hollow trunks, underneath roofs or in between rocks.

Some birds make do with a crack in the ground which they simply cover with straw or twigs. Regardless of how the actual structure of these nests appears, they provide a safe haven in dangerous, hostile environments. It usually takes ten to fifty days before the eggs hatch, which gives the ever-present predators plenty of opportunity to seek and destroy them. During this time, parents take turns in covering their eggs. In birds of prey, it is exclusively the female that cares for them. Sometimes parents will part immediately after their babies emerge from the eggs. Several days prior to the actual birth, a squealing will announce that hatching time is near. The mother will then stay with her offspring at all times. The process of breaking the egg is sometimes a real struggle for life. Fortunately for them, the newborns have a hard, sharp growth on top of their beaks which helps them to break the hard shell. Being subsequently useless, this tool then gradually disappears. Most bird species take great care of the nests, for example regularly cleaning them of excrement and dirt.

Depending on whether they belong to the group of altricial or precocial animals, young birds may take their time before leaving the nest or, in the latter case, are capable of leaving the nest very quickly. If they hesitate, their parents encourage them with special noises while standing in front of them with food in their beaks. They walk backwards and forwards and keep on repeating these movements

Born in a nest

until the young birds finally decide to leave the nest. Sometimes, more bird species will make use of the same nest and alter it according to their needs and instincts.

In late winter, when the storks return from their long journeys, the male begins his search for the nest he was born in. As soon as he finds it, he

starts on the reconstruction works: he adds extra twigs to make it larger and more robust and lays moss and straw on the bottom to reinforce its structure. After several years, some of these nests may weigh more than 1000 pounds! A few days later, when all is ready, the female arrives. After mating, which takes place in early spring, the females usually lay four eggs. The incubation period takes ten days and at the end of it the young storks are born. They hatch one after another over a period of four weeks. Immediately after the first egg has been laid, the parents start taking turns sitting on their precious eggs.

For stork parents, the first three weeks are the most challenging. To satisfy their voracious babies' appetite they need to bring massive quan-

tities of food which they disgorge in the center of the nest. Once this initial period is over, the already-feathered fledglings start beating their wings. However, it is two months after birth before the young storks are able to fly out of their nest. Then, during this first phase of independent existence in the world, the parents continue feeding them as the young ones return to the nest every night. After some time, the young birds are ready to leave the nest for good. A short time later the parents, together with their offspring, set off on a long and demanding journey to the African continent. Three years later, by that time fully-grown adults, the stork adolescents return to the land of their birth to nest there just as their parents did. In Western culture, the stork is seen as a portent of a good home and childbirth: it is said that storks delivers babies to homes, carrying them in their beaks, and are thus seen as a symbol of childbirth. Thanks to this alleged social role, the stork has always held the sympathy and protection of humans.

[1-2] The nest of the great crested grebe is made mostly of algae. Adult birds bring the algae to a shallow nest and use it to cover up their eggs whenever they have to leave them unattended. When the fledglings hatch, both males and females feed their babies. [3-4-5-6] Stork nests are wide and are built high above the ground. In cities and towns, you will often find them on top of old smoke-stacks that are no longer used.

[1] Within 2–3 days, the female common buzzard will lay 3–4 eggs in its nest. When, from time to time, it leaves the nest, the role of guardian is taken over by the male who is, under normal circumstances, responsible for feeding her while she sits on her eggs.

[2] The moorhen usually builds its nest amongst the reeds close to water, however sometimes it makes use of a squirrel's home and builds its nest in a tree trunk.

[3] The osprey is a bird of prey which hunts fish. It therefore quite logically always makes its nest somewhere near water.

[4] The nest of the common shag is built on a rock on the edge of a cliff.

[5] The female and male of the lesser noddy keep watch together over their nest.
[6] With their hungry bills wide open, the fledglings of the red-backed shrike are waiting for food.
[7] The Eurasian kestrel does not really build a nest, instead laying its egg into a hollow in a tree or in a brick wall, on a ledge or even in an old, abandoned nest of a raven or a magpie.

[1-2] The nest of the roseate spoonbill is made of woven reeds or willow wicker. The male and female take turns attending to their infants. Their plumage quickly changes from pure white to bright pink.

[1-2-3] The Great tit builds its nest in a hole in a tree or in a wall; twice a year it lays 5–12 eggs there. The incubation takes thirteen days. The young birds leave their nest around twenty days after hatching.

[4] The nest of the black-necked grebe lays hidden in the reeds.
[5] Little sparrow hawks are waiting for their parents who have left them alone to search for food.
[6] The common buzzard often builds its nest in trees or on cliffs.

[1] The spherical nest of the Taveta Golden weaverbird can only be accessed from below.

[2] The marabou storks nest in large colonies, very often together with pelicans.

[3] After birth, young long-eared owls are covered with grey, fluffy down.

[Right] The Golden oriole builds its nest on treetops and lays three to five eggs there. Fledglings live on a diet of berries.

Of all monkeys, the Japanese
macaque lives furthest north.
It is resistant to the cold
mainly thanks to its thick fur.

The intense cold in the Arctic region causes the sea to freeze and creates a solid layer of ice up to several yards thick. This frozen wasteland is a temporary as well as a permanent habitat to all sorts of animals that are, in one way or another, capable of surviving in such harsh conditions: polar bears, walruses, grey seals, ivory gulls, snowy owls and many others. All these give birth to their young in this hostile and tough environment.

The tundra which surrounds the Arctic, with its permanently frozen subsoil, is home to musk-ox, caribou and reindeer which come there in summer to mate and give birth. Lemmings, on the other hand, live there permanently. They dig burrows in the snow and give birth there.

The Antarctic, a continent within the Antarctic Circle covered in snow and a thick layer of ice which can be as much as 27 feet thick on the surface but is in fact over a mile thick in some places, is located around the South Pole. Among other animals, this inhospitable part of the world provides the natural habitat for penguins and albatrosses. They live in the coastal regions. Animals living there avoid the central parts of the continent where the conditions are far too harsh even for them. The summer is very short in both the Arctic and the Antarctic regions. Some animal populations go there in summertime with only one goal: to mate and reproduce. There is food and a scarcity of predators around – a guarantee that their young have a fair chance of safely surviving the early stages of their life.

When the winter sets in, some species stay there. Their thick fur and subcutaneous fatty tissue protects them against the extremely harsh climatic conditions. Others leave for more hospitable areas, returning the following summer to the same places. The positions of the sun, the moon and the stars help them to find their way in this barren land.

Young animals born on the ice must definitely grow and develop very rapidly because favorable weather lasts only a very short time. They have to be strong enough to face and survive the extreme

Born in wintertime

winters or else they have to migrate to warmer areas. Other animals have to condition themselves to life in the high mountains. Nothing grows on the bare mountain ridges and so if they want to find food they have to descend to lower altitudes. That is exactly what many herbivores do. They are followed by carnivores such as leopards and lynx that prey on the small, weak and vulnerable.

1 **2**

3 [1-7] Thanks to its perseverance, strength and extreme resistance to low temperatures, the Canadian husky is the best sled-dog in the world. Without any difficulty, bitches give birth in the cold snow. These dogs are most at home in an environment where temperatures drop as low as 32 °F and would definitely not be happy inside your house kept as pets, which is unfortunately very often the case.

[1-4] The Sika deer occur mainly in China and Japan and are certainly not afraid of the cold. In March, following their birth, antlers of six to eight horns grow upon their head. There are several known subspecies and cross-breeds.

[5-7] Young cougars love playing in the snow.
[6] The thick fur of the European bison is
the best protection against the cold.

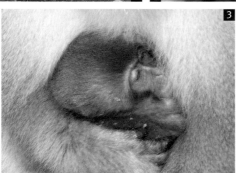

3 [1-6] The Japanese macaques seem to be completely indifferent to cold and frost. However, when it gets too cold for them, they go bathing in hot springs to warm up. The largest population of macaques lives on the plateau of Shiga which is part of the Joshinetsu Kogen National Park in Japan.

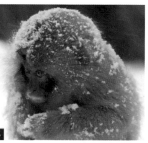

Birth

[1-3] A female Black-legged kittiwake sitting with its back against the wind to protect its fledglings from a cold blizzard.

[2-6] Only during the sunny hours of the day does a young penguin dare to stray far from its mother.

[4-7-8] The Magellanic penguin owes
its name to the famous scientist
and explorer who discovered this
animal in Tierra del Fuego.
[5] The lifespan of the Hooded seal
can be as much as forty years.
If it lives to see that age, it may
weigh as much as 1000 pounds.

63

[1] From a very early age, the cougar is capable of following animal tracks in the snow.
[2] The snow leopard, or ounce, lives in mountainous areas of the Himalaya mountain range. The female gives birth to between two and five cubs in a den which is usually situated in a rocky crevice. The young animals live with their mother for one whole year.

The animal kingdom comprises countless species and is characterized by immense diversity. A unicellular organism and a mammal of course do not have much in common.

And yet each and every species has its typical physical features, its habits and specific patterns of behaviour. Some very simple animals still surprise us by their unexpected capabilities and others by their rather bizarre exteriors. In all categories there are species which may in their own way aspire to be listed in the record books. They are all unique and special in one way or another. Let us mention for example the blue whale, one of the largest and heaviest animals to have ever existed on Earth. At birth, a baby blue whale weighs two metric tonnes and is approximately 23 feet long. Upon reaching maturity, it will weigh more than 130 metric tonnes. In 1947, a specimen was caught which weighed an unbelievable 190 tonnes, the equivalent of thirty-one elephants.

The longest animal in the world is the sea worm. When looking for great jumpers, apart from the bullfrog we must not forget about the flea. It can jump as high as 8 inches which is 150 times its length.

Many infant animals are killed by their predators or die as result of a disease. Some animals, such as the Caddis Fly, are programmed to live for only a short time, while the lifespan of others is very long. The Galapagos Giant Turtle can live more than 150 years and females of a killer whale can live to see one full century.

However, there are still other, perhaps even more interesting records worth mentioning. The Pacific Golden Plovers cover more than 11,000 miles every year back and forth between Brazil and Canada in search of food. The Green Turtle on the other hand can swim almost 1,900 miles only to

The largest and smallest of insects and invertebrates

reach a series of tiny islands in the middle of the Pacific Ocean where it mates and reproduces. Then it undertakes the same journey in the opposite direction only to return to the Brazilian coast. Unlike reptiles, fish, birds and mammals, the

[1] The Colorado potato beetle, imported to Europe from the American continent along with potatoes, is a much feared parasite which can cause great damage to this vegetable. In particular its larvae, which eat the leaves, are considered to be a great nuisance for agriculture.

invertebrates do not have an inner vertebra, or backbone. Invertebrates represent 95 percent of all living species, from amoeba and insects, to jellyfish, worms, spiders, and the crustacean and mollusc families. They can be found literally everywhere: in water and air, as well as on the land. The number of insect species is breathtaking. They are immensely diverse in shape, color and size. And they are extremely effective at reproducing. For example, a queen termite lays eggs every two seconds, around the clock.

Insects lay their eggs in very diverse environments – some lay eggs on leaves, some into the ground, still others lay their eggs onto the stems of various plants which then provide their larvae with the required nutrition. Through a gradual metamorphosis they reach their final form of life. Some species live for only a few hours. That is, however, long enough for them to mate, lay eggs and thus preserve the natural cycle of life. Spiders, for example, lay eggs in cocoons underneath stones or the bark of some trees.

Crustacean eggs float around freely in water or are attached underneath the female's tail. The eggs are laid or released in different stages of their development. The pink prawn lays billions of eggs which produce microscopic larvae which bear almost no resemblance to the adult animal. A crayfish larva, on the other hand, is very much like an adult crustacean immediately after it leaves the egg.

There are more than 45,000 known species of mollusc which differ from one another not only in their morphology but also in their behavior. Most, such as clams and octopi, live in water, while others, for instance snails and slugs, live on dry land. These lay their eggs in prepared holes in the ground. A month or so later, a tiny snail comes out, with the beginnings of a shell on its back. Some time later, they leave their nests in search of food. Their journey puts them at risk of numerous dangers from predators and birds.

[2] The larvae of the Caddis fly live in water in a cocoon of vegetable residue.

[3-4] The nest of the Paper wasp is made of wood which is first processed by the insects and made into a matter similar to papier-mâché (a material which consists of pieces of paper mixed with glue).

[5] The egg case is a type of cocoon containing the eggs. Here we can see the egg case of a preying mantis.

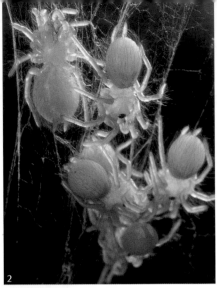

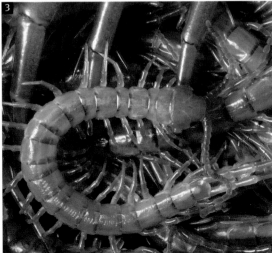

[1-2] The body of a young tarantula is almost transparent and gradually becomes covered with many stinging hairs.
[3] The gigantic centipedes (*scolopendra*) native to the island of Martinique, among others, move around by means of their many green legs.

4 5

[4] A young stick insect looks much like a strangely animated twig.
[5] The Emperor scorpion is a feared predator which does not hesitate to attack snakes, rodents or lizards.
[6] The larvae of the cockchafer spread true terror among gardeners. They are armed with small jaws which can bite and destroy stems as well as the roots of garden plants.

6

[1] This gigantic hairy spider is only a baby tarantula. Adult females are larger than males and they also live longer: 20 years for females as compared to 5 years for males.
[2] These erect, tiny larvae will metamorphose into splendid Camberwell beauty butterflies.

[1] During a dive, the Peregrine falcon reaches speeds of more than 180 miles per hour. This immense speed makes it the fastest bird in the world.

[2-3-4] With a height of 9 feet, the ostrich is the largest of all birds. It has a top speed of 40 mph making it the fastest bird on land. It also holds another record: its eggs are by far the largest: they weigh more than 3 pounds.

[1] A sloth breaks all records in idleness: it needs approximately one hour to crawl a distance of 330 feet (or 100 metres).
[2] There are many different species of chameleon. Infants are no bigger than a raspberry.

[3] The giraffe is the tallest of all land animals, with heights exceeding 15 feet.
[4] The sea-elephant is the largest of all palmipeds. Males can grow up to 23 feet long.
[5] The harvest mouse is the smallest rodent. A fully grown individual does not weigh more than a mere 0.2 ounces (6 grams).

First steps

A baby llama can stand up on its own within an hour of coming into the world. It is even able to run short distances.

After birth, the babies of some animals are defenseless. They depend fully on the care and protection of their parents. Others come into the world more or less ready and capable, usually after a long period of gestation. When born they have hair or fur, relatively strong muscles and alert senses.

In a way, they are independent even though they still depend on their mothers' care and feeding. Large herbivorous animals (draft horses for example) usually live in herds. Even though they lack coordination and stability to begin with, they are capable of standing up and walking almost immediately after birth and to a certain extent they can keep up with the normal behavior of the adult animals which surround them. This initial mobility is vitally important for survival. The young one must be up and walking as soon as possible so as to be able to follow the mother or to become part of the herd which provides them with protection. Only in this way do they have a chance to avoid predators which very often choose the easy prey of the young and the ill. There is barely anywhere to hide

in the wide open spaces of the savannah where wild beasts roam in search of prey. To be able to provide enough food, a herd must start moving immediately after the birth of the young.

The amount of time baby animals are given to stand up and start walking differs substantially among species. A fawn, for instance, has a fair chance of going unnoticed thanks to its camouflage of spots which enables it to blend in with the background and it can therefore wait several days before standing up. An antelope is standing less than an hour after birth, as soon as its mother licks it clean.

After birth, birds are just as vulnerable and defenceless as some mammals. To survive they need the care and protection that only their parents can

Premature babies

give them. They remain stuck in their nests, nervously awaiting the arrival of their parents who provide food. Generally speaking, most songbirds are altricials. Other young birds are far more developed and therefore also independent: they stay in the nest for only a few hours or several hours at most. When they are born, they already have rela-

tively thick, fluffy down and are able to move about and search for food on their own. Ducklings can hear and see immediately after birth and they also have an adult plumage. They leave the nest, waddle behind their mother and soon they can even swim. They are referred to as precocial animals. These baby birds often find themselves abandoned before they have time to mature. The parents quickly sense the moment when they are not needed any longer and simply abandon them to their fate.

There are bird species, however, which are somewhere between the strong, precocial, and the weak, altricials. Let us, as an example, mention owls and herons: their young enter the world with a thick plumage and open eyes, yet they are dependent on their parents until they learn how to fly. Birds of prey are born with near

perfect, high quality feathers but they remain blind for several days. They leave their nest five to ten days before they are able to fly and so for a few days they sit on the branches of surrounding trees puzzling over the problem of flying.

[1-6] The goslings of the Grey Lag goose are born yellow, only gradually turning grey. Some time before the beginning of winter, the fledglings born in the spring become capable of following their parents on their long, challenging journeys to the south in search of warmth and food.

[1] A baby zebra can walk and follow its mother within two hours of birth.
[2] The foal of this English thoroughbred can gallop at full speed on the same day that it is born.

[1-2] A female elephant is helping its newborn baby to stand up.

[3] A young, white rhino is still being nursed by its mother, however, at the same time it is already learning to eat grass, which distinguishes it from the African black rhinoceros which lives off a diet of leaves.

[4-6] The Blue wildebeest is on the alert from the moment it comes into the world. It keeps a watch out for large carnivores. [5] The European bison is capable of following its herd one hour after birth.

[1-2] A baby hippopotamus can swim before it can walk. It rests on the water's surface, lying on its mother's back.

[3-4] A baby dromedary does not leave its mother. She is there to support the young animal on its still uncertain and shaking legs.
[5] The infants of the Spectacled Caimans rush into the water immediately after birth.

[1] The young puma, or cougar as it is often called, does not roar. Instead it makes purring noises. It leaves its mother's womb with well-developed sight which enables it to detect prey in the wide open plains of the American West.
[2] If it does not want to be abandoned by the herd, the baby buffalo has to be able to stand up on its own only a few minutes after birth.
[3-4] Shortly after birth, a wild boar piglet can stand on its own.
[5] A baby camel can keep up with the rest of the group less then two hours after being thrown into the harsh world of the desert.

After 14 months of gestation a giraffe produces a single infant. Occasionally there may be two animals in one litter.

At birth, a baby giraffe drops to solid ground from a height of approximately six feet. This is because its mother stands with her hind legs splayed as she gives birth. The baby can do one thing only – absorb the shock with its front legs.

Half an hour later, the giraffe infant is standing on its still trembling legs and begins to suckle. The mother cleans and smells her baby and uses her head to push it towards her teats. The following morning, the young animal is already up and running around, and on the third day it is stable and mobile enough to start learning how to jump and run quickly. It is in fact a perfect small-scale copy of its mother with long legs, the typical long neck and patterns on its body. This camouflage remains unchanged in the future. A baby giraffe is six feet tall and soon enough it is able to reach the branches of trees where it finds its favourite diet, the leaves of the acacia tree. For the time being though, it is happy with grass and its mother's highly nutritious milk. It continues to suckle until the age of nine months.

If necessary to protect its young one, the mother places it between her front legs and starts kicking her strong hind legs wildly in all directions. This usually works as protection against the ever-present hungry predators. Sometimes though, the mother leaves her baby together with other young giraffes on a remote, elevated place where its camouflage means it can pass unnoticed. The mother observes from a distance. Approximately fifty percent of all young giraffes die soon after birth, usually within one year. Mostly they are

A gangly baby giraffe

killed by lions, cheetahs and leopards. This high mortality rate is partly compensated for by the giraffes' high fertility rate. They give birth every 20–23 months. Female giraffes reach sexual maturity at the age of three years and then remain fertile until the age of twenty.

[1] The giraffe is a very attentive mother. It takes great cares for its young and, when necessary, is ready to defend it with great determination.
[2] From a very early age, giraffes can graze on not only grass but also on the twigs and branches of African acacia trees which are literally covered in thorns.
[3] The young animal leaves its mother's protection after approximately sixteen months.

[4] At birth, a baby giraffe weighs approximately 130 pounds; an adult animal can weigh more than a metric tonne.

[5] After one week, small horns covered with black fur begin to grow on the infant's head. They remain for the rest of the animal's life.

95

[1] A mother helping her baby to stand up. If the young
one does not succeed in getting up within an hour
of birth, the other giraffes usually leave it alone and,
inevitably, it becomes prey for the large carnivores.
[2] Female giraffes live in groups where each individual
supervises and cares for its own infant.

The Reticulated and the Rothschild's giraffe are subspecies differentiated by the pattern of their spots. In total, there are eight subspecies of giraffe.

T he infants of many animals grow up in nests and dens while others are carried around by their mothers. Some are able to walk on their own after a couple of days while others need several weeks just to stand up.

Even though they can move around on their own, these baby animals cling to their mothers' bodies: monkeys and marsupials are good examples of this type of animal group. Carrying your baby around is not only practical – the close contact with its mother's body gives the young animal a feeling of security and often also teaches it vitally important lessons for future life. A baby kangaroo settles in its mother's pouch where it stays for more than six months. Only occasionally does it dare to leave the warm and cosy "pocket." Baby kangaroos leave the pouch for good at eight months old. Monkeys are another good example: baby monkeys' arms and legs are strong, so before they learn to walk they cling to their mother's fur on her stomach. A little bat wraps its wings around its mother's body and takes one of the fake teats into its mouth. Sticking firmly to her body, they leave together in search of insect prey. Many animal species carry the young on their backs. Monkeys do this as soon as their babies are old enough but this is also the means of transportation for American anteater infants. Some baby monkeys wrap their arms around the mother's back and roll their tails around the mother's tail. Even though some water fowl hatchlings spend their early days on the mother's back, they usually only do this to rest, when they become too tired to continue swimming. Some lower animal species carry their young until they become strong enough to defend themselves independently of their parents. Thanks to its uniquely

The luxury of being carried

shaped legs and suckers, a newborn scorpion can enjoy the luxury of being carried around on its mother's back for three to fifteen days. Then the infant temporarily leaves its parent to try hunting under supervision. Afterwards it returns, continuing until it is ready to live the independent life of an adult scorpion.

[1-2] A she-wolf is carrying her pups in her mouth. The young wolves willingly submit themselves to this mode of transportation.
[3] The Ring-tailed lemur clings firmly to its mother's back.
[4] Female toads can lay 50–70 eggs which are then fertilized by the male. The fertilized eggs are then carried wrapped around the hind legs until they hatch.

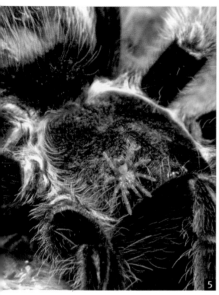

[5] With its almost transparent body, a tiny baby tarantula hides on its mother's back. It is resistant to the effect of the stinging hairs which are erect whenever the spider becomes stressed or feels in danger.
[6] The Emperor scorpion carries its young on its back avoiding anything that would want to attack and eat them.
[7] Just like many other mammal species, the Laughing hyena carries its newly-born babies in its mouth.

3 [1-2-3] Female anteaters usually have only one baby. They then continue carrying it on the back for almost a year, despite the fact that the infant is capable of walking as young as four weeks old. In this manner, anteaters protect their young against the danger of pumas and jaguars.

[4] A baby chameleon very often stays on its mother's body. It cannot yet change color and pattern as quickly as an adult chameleon and cannot therefore use its camouflage techniques to blend in with its surroundings.

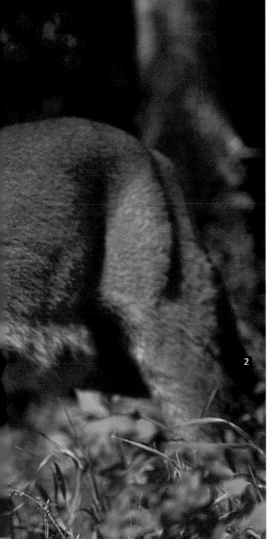

[1] A lioness always carries her cubs around in her mouth to protect them from hyenas.
[2] A baby cougar is often carried in its mother's mouth across vast distances.

[1] Clinging to its mother's back, a baby Ring-tailed lemur learns to distinguish edible leaves from harmful ones. In the near future, this skill will become essential for finding food.

[2] For long months, the babies of the Verreaux's sifaka stay on her mother. They come off only for a few hours a day to play around with other young animals from the same group.

[3] A little Rhesus macaque is carried by its mother, to whose stomach it clings.

[4] Sitting on its mother's or father's shoulders, a baby orangutan is exploring its future territory.
[5-6] The female Barbary macaque monkey takes an active part in the upbringing of her young while it is not unusual to see males carrying babies around.

4

5

6

[1-3] Little Geladas cling to their mother's fur and hold fast so as not to fall off accidentally.
[2] A young gibbon hides underneath its mother's stomach.

4 5

[4-5] Baby chimpanzees just love to be carried around on their mother's back. They continually get on and off during a day full of action. [6] Baboons never leave their young alone on the ground where they would sooner or later fall victim to predators, especially to lionesses. [7] During the mating period, female Barbary macaque monkeys will mate with more than one male. The babies do not know which is their father, though this does not prevent them from climbing onto the backs of the males.

6

7

In some animals, growth and development proceeds with a more or less continuous rhythm. The body changes though it remains quite similar to its initial shape and form: bones grow in length, muscles grow in strength and quite quickly the young animal achieves the form and abilities of the adult.

Then as the animal matures sexually, its growth slowly stops. In the early stages of its life, it resembles its parents; though much smaller, it is in some sense a copy. This manner of development is common to all vertebrates.

A baby giraffe resembles its mother, just as a young elephant or foal looks very much like its parents. In other animals, the initial fur disappears, to be replaced by a different one. This is the case for baby penguins and seal pups. In other animals, to fully develop their exterior must undergo a profound change which may then last throughout the rest of their life. Lizards and reptiles grow mainly as a result of these constant and profound changes. The shell of a crustacean must first crack before it hardens again, thus creating a new shell.

A prawn changes its shape several times before it matures.

However, certain species must undergo a total metamorphosis before they become what they are meant to be. After birth, or hatching, these animals are anything but identical to their parents. A tadpole does not have the lungs that a fully developed frog has; the larvae of many insects have neither wings nor legs and essentially, a caterpillar has nothing in common with the beauty and elegance of a butterfly.

The life of a butterfly consists of four different stages: first, there is an egg out of which a larva hatches. The larva (or nymph) takes the form of a caterpillar. The caterpillar must then pupate to reach the final stage of its growth, in insects commonly called an imago. As for the length of the individual stages, that differs from one butter-

Growing, changing, metamorphosing

fly species to another. Some complete their metamorphosis in a course of several weeks, while others need years. Butterflies often lay more than a thousand eggs, usually close to plants which subsequently serve as food for the caterpillars.

[1] This green tree python (amethystine python) will lose its bright yellow skin. It will be replaced by a green one.

However, only a limited number live to see the end of the whole cycle. Caterpillars hatch from eggs, usually laid in autumn, sometimes in early spring. The caterpillar then breaks the shell, sometimes with great difficulty, and crawls out head first. Immediately after getting out, it starts eating the shell of the egg which contains nutrition-rich substances which are vital for the caterpillar's initial survival. Despite what many of us might think, a caterpillar's body is quite a complex machine and it is in fact a fully autonomous animal in its own right. Caterpillars grow very quickly: the skin stretches, cracks and peels off only to be replaced by a new, larger one. To complete the metamorphosis, at the end of which it becomes a butterfly, the body needs oxygen and sufficient nutrition. Some grow and remain hidden in leaves; other caterpillars spend most of their time in the sun. Caterpillars are rarely safe: they often fall prey to birds which feed them to their fledglings, or to certain mammals or other insect species. They have quite intricate methods of defence: some use camouflage, others stick to poisonous plants and adopt their colours to repel predators, still others are able to "jump" to the ground in case of emergency. As soon as a caterpillar eventually reaches its final size, it grips onto a stem or the underside of a leaf. Its skin then cracks and a cocoon slowly emerges. It remains in this form for several weeks or even months until a butterfly crawls out of it.

[2] When leaving its nest, the Eurasian kestrel has a plumage of white, fluffy down.
[3] This tiny tadpole will become a frog.
[4] A baby King Penguin appears larger than its parents.
[5] The Leopard gecko will go through a number of profound changes in its life.

[1-4] The fur of a young wild boar has bright stripes. As the wild boar piglet grows older, the pattern disappears. [5-8] A baby tapir also has white stripes on its coat. Its hair will later turn pitch black.

Before a caterpillar of the Rusty Tussock moth
(or Vapourer moth) reaches the stage of an imago,
it is covered with yellow bristles which are designed
to deter birds.

The arctic fox cub changes its fur during the first winter
of its life. The fur becomes white, the same color and hue
as freshly fallen snow which covers the land all around.

[1] The caterpillar of the Cabbage white butterfly is a garden vegetable parasite.
[2] The caterpillar of the Purple tiger butterfly is armed with very effective stinging hairs.
[3-5-7] The chrysalis of the Common crow (also called the Oleander butterfly) is known for its distinctive sparkling, silvery appearance and in the sun it resembles a piece of jewellery hanging from a branch.
[4] As their bodies are poisonous, caterpillars of the Death's-head moth do not need to fear anything.

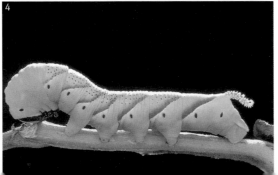

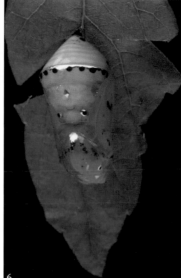

[6] The Plain tiger butterfly (*danaus chrysippus Linnaeus*) and its golden larvae often resemble jewellery hanging from leaves.
[8] Caterpillars of the Eyed hawk-moth (*smerinthus ocellata*) try to intimidate birds by displaying a spike similar to a sharp thorn.

3 [1-3] A caterpillar first needs to pupate into a chrysalis before it can proceed further and metamorphose into this splendid Blue Morpho butterfly.

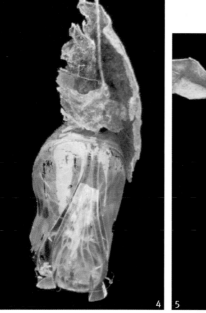

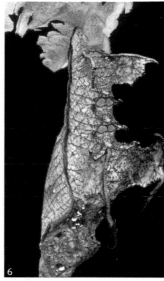

[4-5] The body of this transparent chrysalis is opening so that a beautiful butterfly can be born.
[6] Some larvae look just like leaves, which ensures they go unnoticed by hungry predators.
[7] Caterpillars of the Lackey moth are voracious. It takes them less then a month to eat the leaves off an entire tree.

Life on earth originated in water and for many million years life remained and developed there alone. Some animals, such as fish, and some insect species such as the Backswimmer, together with some lower forms of life such as mollusks, jellyfish and crustaceans have remained there until this day, never venturing onto dry land.

Other species gradually emerged from the depths, leaving the oceans to explore and settle ashore. Since then certain animal species have lived double lives. Most vertebrates which live in water do, from time to time, take to the land. Sea mammals, for example, divide their time unevenly between land and water. In water they are much more adept and agile though. Whales, of course, never leave the ocean and neither do dugongs or manatees. Some animals, on the other hand, take to the water to give birth or come ashore for the same reason.

Penguins, albatrosses, turtles and crocodiles all lay their eggs on dry land. This is not a bad idea

A female hippopotamus has two udders which are both placed very low on her body. When it is submerged in water, the young animal must hold its breath and drink its mother's milk under the surface.

since it is far from simple to incubate an egg in water. Several bird species such as the swan, the gannet and the gull live both in water and on land. Some young animals can swim after birth but others need their parents' assistance to leave the dry land. A seal pup must dive into the ice-cold ocean to find food while a young hippopotamus must enter the water to cool its skin so as not to get a fever from the heat of the fierce African sun. A baby otter, on the other hand, will not go into the water unless its mother literally forces it to do so. She does this when the baby is one month old. By that time the fur of the infant has become sufficiently water-proof.

When the female Harp seal feels that the time to give birth has arrived, it begins to search for a place where the coastal ice crust is thick enough

In water and on dry land

to carry it while it gives birth to its pup.

If she chose thin ice, she would risk the life of her pup. At birth it is very well protected by a thick, white coat of fur. Unable to move, the pup stays put, lying on the ice for approximately ten days. During this initial stage it either sleeps or suckles milk. To be able to survive in the extreme weather

conditions, the pup must quickly grow larger and stronger – its mother's highly nutritious, fatty milk is in fact the only chance for survival for the helpless pup. This life-giving drink allows the young one to build up energy supplies in the form of subcutaneous fatty tissue. As result of lactating, the mother rapidly loses weight because it stops eating for the time it nurses its infant. And so the pup grows fat and strong. If all goes well, two weeks after birth the pup will weigh more than 60 pounds.

After this initial period, the mother abruptly abandons its pup and returns to the group of adult seals. The abandoned pups, huddling desperately together, cry continuously for several days. Once they calm down, a period of fasting and nervous expectations begins. After two weeks, the pups lose their immaculately white fur. By the time this is over and the pup finally makes the decision to dive into the water and find some food, the pup will have lost more than 30 pounds of weight. The pup must try hard to get into the water. The ice is slippery and the seal pup is still very inexperienced in its movements. To begin with, it swims rather clumsily: it cannot swim and stay underwater so it eats only small crustaceans which float on the surface. As an adult, it will be able to move around swiftly with great skill, thanks to the aerodynamic shape of its body in combination with very strong hind legs which are webbed. When they reach one year of age, seal pups set out on a long journey. The seal pups must head north alone. During their two and a half month long trip they cover a distance of around 1,800 miles. Eventually they find and join the community of adult seals.

[1] A seal pup is also sometimes called a whitecoat – due to its typical thick, snow-white fur.

[2] A seal pup cannot swim.
[3] At birth, a pup is approximately 33 inches long; during nursing, which lasts for ten days, it gains on average 5 and a half pounds a day.
[4] At the beginning of its active life, a seal pup lives off crabs and mollusks; a grown animal devours more than 10 pounds of fish a day.
[5] The mother can recognise its young one by its scent.

[1-2-3] Galapagos sea lion pups having a good time ashore on a pleasant, sunny day. They sprawl in the sun, and only dive into the water to cool themselves down.

[4] This sea elephant pup does not yet have the typical bump on its head; in adulthood, it will be there to impress other males.

128

[5] Immediately after being weaned, the hooded seal pup must leave the coastal ice flow and dive into the water in search of food.
[6] The Northern gannet always stays close to the shore.
[7] The Harp seal does not feel at ease on the ice where it can move at a maximum speed of 1 mile per hour. Once in the water it can swim at speeds as high as 25 miles per hour.

[1-4] Galapagos sea lions mate in water. The female gives birth to its young on land where, shortly before her time comes, she retires to a well-chosen place. At birth, a young pup weighs around 25 pounds. A year later, it will be an impressive 44-66 pounds.

[5-8] A sea lion mother and pup recognise each other by voice and scent. The pup will continue to be nursed for one year, and then it will be left to its fate. An orphan does not stand a chance because all other nursing females will reject it.

[1] When mallard ducks are not flying, they spend their day on the water.

[2] The typical pink color of the flamingo is caused by its diet. They live in brackish waters and hunt for a particular prawn species called *artemia salina*, also known as the Brine shrimp. These organisms also cause the coloring of salt marshes, their primary habitat.

[3] A young Red-eared terrapin can only survive close to water.

[4] In summer, Barnacle geese live on the cliffs and rocks of islands in the Arctic region. In winter, they live on coastal flooded meadows and marshes, on the shores of bays and at low tide they can also be found on shallow muddy ground.

[5] The raccoon is an excellent swimmer. On dry land, it is more vulnerable and so it often resorts to tree tops where it perches on branches.
[6] The baby Western Whip snake often find cover in lily flowers where it hunts for prey in the form of various insects.
[7] Otters mate in water. After sixty days, a female gives birth to 1, 2 or 3 babies.

[1-4] Hippopotamuses are most at home in water. When submerged, their immense body weight becomes more tolerable. For as long as fifteen minutes, these animals can remain in a state of apnea.

137

Some animal species have disappeared abruptly from the face of Earth due to natural disasters. Others have become extinct only gradually, mainly because they could not adapt to changes in their environment. Since the Middle Ages, animal species have been disappearing more and more rapidly.

The Giant Panda has been declared a national treasure by the Chinese government. In 1949, it became the symbol of the World Wide Fund for Nature (WWF). It is a critically endangered species – these days, there are only 900 animals living in the wild.

Over the course of three centuries, more than four hundred different species have become extinct, mainly as a result of substantial changes to their environment and excessive hunting by humans. In every natural environment there are complex and interconnected food chains. Some animals play the role of predator while at the same time being the prey of other animals. Baby animals are of course easy prey; however there are many other threats apart from predatory attack which are a danger to an animal species as a whole. In order to acquire land, people destroy tropical forests. The destruction of vegetation which provides a natural habitat for animals inevitably means their gradual extinction. Where can a female find the leaves vital to her survival as well as that of her young? The destruction of swamps, glades and marshes has resulted in the disappearance of colonies of alligators, manatees and water birds. Chemical and radioactive waste pollutes air, land and water, while small amounts build up in animals' bodies and slowly but surely poison them. DDT, a strong insecticide, causes serious changes in bird egg shells which become too delicate and crack easily. This has resulted, for example, in a dramatic decrease in the population of the Brown pelican on the coast of Latin America. They were affected by the poisons present in the fish, their main food source. Apart from this, people continue to hunt endangered species in order to produce such luxury goods as furs, leather, rare exotic foods etc. In order to satisfy tourists and collectors, today more than ever before, poachers are active. They are after eggs, precious feathers, rhino horns, baby animals. They will take anything of value on the

Animals in danger

black market. Fortunately, countries across the world have been implementing new laws and introducing measures aimed at the protection of animals. More and more species are being included on endangered animal lists. Many species reproduce in captivity – in zoos and nature reserves. Some of the young animals are then returned to their natural habitats.

[1] As they try to cross roads, wild boar piglets are often killed by cars and trucks.

[2-3] In the past, the Hermann tortoise used to be a commodity of intense trading. They were often sold as pets. Fortunately, trade in these animals has been made illegal.

[4] Orangutans only live on the island of Borneo in the dense rainforests: however, these forests are shrinking every day, resulting in a reduction of the natural habitat of these apes.

[5] Nowadays, black leopards have nearly become extinct in the wild.

[6] Spectacled caimans used to be killed for their skin and today they are strictly protected.

4

5

6

[1-2 & right] The Verreaux's sifakas, just like all other members of the lemur family, live in only one place on earth, in Madagascar. The destruction of the rainforests is nevertheless endangering its existence.
[3] Fawns often fall prey to stray dogs and wolves.

[1] Nowadays, orangutan babies are often born in nature reserves.
[2] Manatees, which some people consider to be behind the legend of the sea sirens and mermaids, are very often killed and maimed by the propellers of ocean liners and other boats.

146

[1-4] Bengal tigers are solitary territorial animals which need a home territory of their own. After mating, the male immediately returns to its territory and does not participate in the upbringing of its cubs. Tiger cubs stay with the mother for a period of two to three years. In the past they were killed for their exotic fur. Today, however, they are strictly protected.

[1-2] During her life, a female orangutan gives birth to only 4–5 young. Once it has been weaned, a baby orangutan stays with its mother until she gives birth to another baby. [3-4] The orangutan is the most endangered of all hominoid apes, its main threat coming from the destruction of the rainforests, its natural habitat. Under current conditions, orangutans are likely to become extinct in the wild within the next fifteen years.

[5] The infants, with look very similar to cute teddy-bears, are hunted, caught and mistreated by poachers who sell them as pets.
[6-8] Females share an area of around 8 square miles, while males live in their own territories, covering about 3 square miles.

After eighteen long months
of gestation, the female
rhinoceros gives birth to
a single infant.

A newborn African (black) rhinoceros enters the world with its eyes wide open, and is capable of standing up on its shaky legs only an hour after birth. Its skin is completely hairless and it does not yet have the typical horns which ironically have become the curse of rhinos.

As the animal grows, the front horn moves further and further back and becomes sharper and sharper. For the first few days, the mother remains hidden with its baby in the undergrowth to minimize any risk of danger. Then they set out on a tour of the territory, the mother leading the young one by means of her horn. A young rhino is very dependant on its mother, for the next few years it follows her everywhere she goes and does not leave her until she gives birth again.

The mother protects the infant from all danger and will attack any threatening predator without hesitation. She is ready to launch a fierce attack upon hearing even the slightest unusual sound. It is not other animals, however, that pose the most serious threat for young rhinos. And it is not lack of food either. As soon as the baby rhino's horn grows, it becomes susceptible to the danger of greedy humans who hunt and kill for this unique kind of bone. It is mainly due to the fact that some people believe that the horn is a strong aphrodisiac. They grind it or use it as material for expensive daggers and ornamental knives. Two or three species of Asian rhino have virtually become extinct due to the intense hunting. African rhinos are protected by law and yet it does not grant them complete safety from hunters and poachers. Moreover, rhinoceroses are not very fertile – they mate only once every three years.

The rhinoceros's horn

Wherever they move, they are always accompanied by a tiny bird, the tick-bird, which helps rid them of parasites. This bird is always alert and therefore warns the animal of any unusual commotion in the vicinity. If a man approaches, the tick bird becomes agitated and the rhino realizes that something is not right.

[1-2] The young rhino basically stays close to its mother at all times; it suckles milk on a regular basis and can drink up to five gallons every day.
[3] Paradoxically, the rhino's horn has virtually led to the extinction of the species as people believed that it is an aphrodisiac.
[4] Rhinos move from place to place mostly in the evenings; in the heat of the midday sun they usually remain still and relax in the shade of large trees.
[5] Immediately after birth, a horn begins growing on the animal's skull. This one will of course grow much bigger and sharper.

[1] A female African black rhinoceros gives birth to a single baby after five hundred long days of gestation.
[2] At birth, a baby rhino weighs 88 pounds. A fully-grown animal can weigh as much as 25 metric tonnes. The African black rhino is an endangered species.

[1] Wherever it goes, the African white rhinoceros is accompanied by tiny tick-birds which remove parasites from its skin.
[2] As a rhino grows, its skin folds in a characteristic fashion, giving the impression that they are covered with armour plating.
[right] Not even the thorniest bushes are safe from the insatiable appetite of the rhinoceros.

3 [1-2-3] Rhinos are in fact placid herbivores; females can nevertheless become enraged when anyone or anything attempts to get close to their young. When taking care of their young, these powerful animals are ready to attack at the slightest sign of danger.

[4] This two year old African black rhinoceros has just been weaned and is beginning its independent existence.

Training
and games

Many wild animals never even catch a glimpse of their parents while others never come into contact with animals of their own kind. And yet, they spontaneously behave as all other animals of their kind. Animals are endowed with a specific amount of genetic information and characteristics which they later pass on to subsequent generations.

For a young animal to become a fully functioning adult, it must go through a phase of learning. When a rabbit is born, it has no idea that a fox is an enemy and that if it spots one it must run away as fast as possible. It acquires this piece of knowledge through observation and experience, sometimes paying for it with its own life. Experience and the imitation of an adult rabbit by the young animal contribute to and enhance its reflexes. It observes and learns from experience: if it makes a mistake, it stores the information in its memory and next time if lucky, solves the given problem. In this way young animals progress through life. This is all possible thanks to its ability to change its beha-

Pogona vitticeps (the Bearded Dragon) is a lizard which can be easily domesticated. It quickly learns to identify the one who feeds it. Animals on sale in pet stores come from breeding stations because this species, native to Australia, is strictly protected.

vioral patterns and thus adapt to new circumstances. All this stimulates intelligence.

For a baby animal, it is not enough to imitate or try things out on its own. The real lessons are learnt from its parents. A monkey, for instance, can guide its baby so that as a result it eats only a particular type of food.

The limits of an individual's ability to learn does, however, depend largely on its genetic makeup – after all, there is no lesson good enough to teach an elephant to fly!

Formative experiences play a crucial role in learning. They strongly influence the future behaviour of the animal. After all, it is life that is at stake here, nothing less. Newborn animals feel an urge

Getting, acquiring, learning

to explore and try everything. As soon as a cub becomes able to leave its den, it immediately begins to explore its surroundings. Everything it sees, hears and smells is stored in its memory. Animals have the ability to remember even though their memory is more limited and far less complex than that of humans.

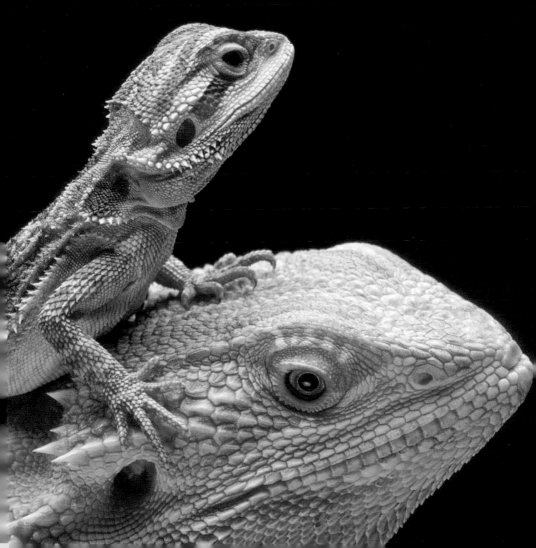

[1] The Leopard gecko learns all its lessons for life through observing and imitating its mother.
[2] This African wild dog puppy learns to hunt in a pack mainly thanks to its observation of the behaviour of the more experienced members of the group.
[3] This Przewalski's horse foal is instinctively heading for its mother's udder.
[4] This donkey foal is busy looking for the tastiest grass.

[5] Lion cubs are learning to hunt through games.
[6] The lioness teaches her cubs to stand downwind so that the prey does not smell them.
[7] Cubs are instinctively driven to kill when they get hungry.

[1] For years, the baby chimpanzee stays with its mother.

[2] An infant always instinctively finds the source of its mother's delicious milk.

[3] From its first days in the world, the young chimpanzee is a mimic. This helps it to clearly express emotions as well as to inform others in the group of its current state of mind.

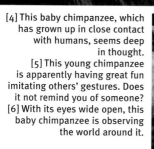

[4] This baby chimpanzee, which has grown up in close contact with humans, seems deep in thought.
[5] This young chimpanzee is apparently having great fun imitating others' gestures. Does it not remind you of someone?
[6] With its eyes wide open, this baby chimpanzee is observing the world around it.

[1] A common snipe trying to take off.
[2-3] Cheetah cubs always learn to hunt from their mother.

[4] A fawn imitating its mother and thus learning how to hide from predators;
no matter what the circumstances, its instincts always tell it to run away from humans.

This chimpanzee mother
will continue to nurse its
baby for several years.

C himpanzees are born blind, hairless, and so weak that they can barely get a grip on their mother's fur. This fragility is compensated for by the fact that a chimpanzee mother continues to take care of its baby for many years, even once the young chimpanzee become stronger and less vulnerable.

Until the age of three, a baby chimpanzee lives in a nest in a tree high above the ground. The mother nurses its baby for a relatively long time, sometimes for a few of years, and does so even after its baby starts eating normal food. A female chimpanzee pays careful attention to her baby, in particular ensuring that other adult members of the group, which as a rule are fascinated by babies, resist the temptation of touching or even stealing her baby.

In the beginning, a baby and its mother create a perfect couple. Most of the time, the female holds her baby tight to her breast and takes it everywhere she goes. A baby chimpanzee sleeps with its mother every night without exception and her arms is the place where the baby relaxes and rests. Together they wake up in the morning and leave the nest in search of food. Chimpanzees love fruits, leaves, eggs and insects, but best of all they like bananas. As soon as a baby becomes capable of swallowing normal food, its mother starts sharing everything with the young chimpanzee.

Within several months a baby ape becomes strong enough to be able to sit astride her mother's back. From that time on, it begins to take a real interest in the world around it, and feels the urge to explore everything.

Up until then, it plays and fools about constantly – mock fighting, romping around, tickling, mutual preening and so on. At first, the baby ape plays with its mother, later with other baby chimpanzees

The lengthy training
of a little chimpanzee

or adults of the same group. Friendships are made which often last for a lifetime. Young chimpanzees enjoy a very long childhood, until the maternal bond abruptly breaks when the individual reaches the age of thirteen.

[1] The childhood of a chimpanzee is very long, lasting over ten years.

[2-3] Young chimpanzees are always busy exploring their surroundings.

[4-5] A baby chimpanzee nibbling at stems and leaves. It could be for fun or simply because it feels like it.

174

[6-7] Leaping from branch to branch is a favourite pastime of chimpanzee babies and adolescents.
[8] At the slightest sign of danger or alarm, young chimpanzees swiftly return to their mother's arms.

175

Even though chimpanzees lack the gift of speech, they use gestures
and mimics as their primary means of communication.

[1] Young chimpanzees are extremely curious.
[2] A chimpanzee baby, clinging to its mother's body, is always sucking on something.
[3] Sometimes you get the impression that chimpanzees are laughing. In reality, however, only humans can laugh.
[right] Chimpanzees love leaping from tree to tree but most of the time they stay on the ground.

[1-3 and left] The various facial mimes of young chimpanzees demonstrate that this ape is the most intelligent of animals.

181

[1-7] Young chimpanzees are excellent climbers; when moving from one branch to another they make use of all four limbs. Leaps are often accompanied by cries of joy and excitement. These are signs of their future fierce territoriality.

3 [1-2-3] Chimpanzees have become a highly valued commodity on the black market. They are sold as pets or, even worse, for meat in some restaurants. [4-5-6] Of all other animals, chimpanzees are closest to humans and can even learn to communicate through sign language invented by humans.

Young carnivores instinctually begin to imitate the hunting behavior of their parents at a very early age. Most vertebrates begin learning by observing their mothers' behavior. The learning period is sometimes very long, some of the young predators eventually becoming terrific hunters and spreading fear and terror wherever they move. However, they kill not for fun but to survive.

Every animal species has its own, varyingly complex techniques and weapons. According to their predispositions, animals develop their own hunting patterns. Mothers teach their young how to hunt their prey, how to get together with other members of the

Hunting

group to increase their power and abilities, how to catch prey in mid-air or how to catch fish in a stream. A jaguar cub learns to lure fish by moving its tongue in the water. A young lynx learns the art of sharpening its senses - staying focused, pricking its ears and identifying its prey by distant sounds at the break of day or at dusk.

When it grows up, this predator can locate its prey at a distance of more than 1000 feet. A panther's mother teaches its cubs two basic modes of hunting - climbing a tree, waiting for the prey there, and jumping down to kill it during the day, or hiding and luring its prey into an ambush on the ground at night. A young crocodile learns to hide in a riverbed and wait until a gazelle comes to drink; a young weasel learns how to slowly approach its prey and then all of a sudden jump and bite it in the neck. Baby spiders learn how to jump into a complex web while a digger wasp must discover that to kill a bee it must sting it under the "chin."

The phase of learning is followed by a phase of practice. In this stage, young animals learn through games how to test their strengths, abilities and the effectiveness of their hunting techniques and movements. Then one day the mother finally lets them hunt. It is not rare for the mother to help its young, for example by not allowing the prey to escape.

[1] A lion cub playing with the shell of a turtle killed by its mother.

[2-4] Cheetahs hunt on the plains, the Thomson gazelle is their favorite prey.

[3] Hyenas, even young ones, will not hesitate to attack large mammals. Often they manage to steal animals which were caught and killed by lions.

[5-6-7] The female lion is usually the family "bread-winner." She usually goes hunting with her weaned cubs.

Even though this Jack Russell Terrier pup is a domesticated animal, its hunting instincts are alive and well.

While she hunts, the cubs closely imitate their mothers' behavior, learning good as well as bad techniques. When the lioness attacks they stay hidden and impatiently await their dinner.

[1-2-3] Foxes have always been considered hen thieves. In reality though, they live mainly on a diet of small rodents, little rabbits and young birds. It is always vixen that teaches its young the art of hunting.

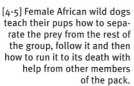

[4-5] Female African wild dogs teach their pups how to separate the prey from the rest of the group, follow it and then how to run it to its death with help from other members of the pack.

A young cheetah cub has keen sight which enables it to see its prey over distances of thousands of feet.

When a cheetah is born, after three months of pregnancy, it does not weigh more than 11 ounces. It is usually accompanied by two or three siblings. It is blind, helpless and completely dependant on its mother's care. She brings up her cubs with surprising commitment. If a cheetah cub is not killed by predators, it grows up to be a strong and much feared hunter.

After approximately ten days, the cub opens its eyes and after three weeks of life it is able to move about with confidence. If a cub tries to stray away from the den, the mother picks it up by the neck and puts it back. She does not let the cub go and play until it is two months old, several weeks before she weans it. A cub has a grey mane around its neck and on its shoulders. This mane disappears after ten weeks and is replaced by the coat of an adult animal. At approximately that time, young cheetahs lose the ability to sheathe their claws, a feature common to all other feline predators. At the age of six months, the mother begins teaching it the art of hunting. A cub observes its mother and thus learns. A female which needs to feed its cubs leaves her den every day to hunt for fresh meat. Cheetahs are not scavengers.

The cub stays with its mother for a long time; in fact it does not leave her until the age of seventeen months. As adults, siblings of one litter will be independent but for some time in the future they will share the prey they kill with the others. Young females then leave the group to begin an indepen-

The cheetah,
the champion of speed

dent life and to mate and reproduce. Once fully grown, the cheetah is the fastest short-distance runner of the savannah. It can achieve speeds of 70 miles per hour, though it can only maintain this immense speed for around a thousand feet.

[1-2-3] It is the female cheetah that does all the hunting. When lying in wait for prey - which can often take a very long time - she either lies on a branch or crouches hidden on the ground. The attack is astonishingly fast, with the top speed of an attacking cheetah reaching well over 60 miles per hour.

[4-5-6] Young cheetah cubs, while continuing to be suckled, do still need fresh meat. A female has to hunt every day while looking after her cubs.

197

Young cheetahs often hunt together. They attack a herd with the goal of separating one individual from the others. One of the cheetahs begins to run after it; it must be very fast because even though cheetahs can run at very high speeds they cannot maintain their speed over long distances.

Fox cubs spend lots of time
playing: their games are in fact
lessons necessary for their
future survival in the wild.

When young mammals don't sleep or eat, they spend their time playing. This is how they learn about life. In the beginning, young animals of the same litter romp around together or with their parents.

Otters love to somersault, leaping and flipping in the air and sliding head over heels down muddy riverbanks. At four months old, a young dolphin will pluck up the courage to leave its mother, and begins to play around with other members of the group.

Even though games are mainly seen as time spent relaxing, there is far more to it than that. Through games, young animals learn to respect and put up with the existence of other animals within or outside their family. When they grapple, fight or romp around they learn their place within the group or community of animals. They test their own strengths and others' weaknesses. They learn to respect the rules of life in a group of animals, its hierarchy as well as boundaries that should not be crossed.

Kittens, just like other baby animals, spend lots of time playing together. They bite, push, they arch their backs and stiffen their tails; they indulge in mock-fights. In reality they learn, clumsily at first but gradually gaining more and more confidence and experience in the various ways of hunting. They use different techniques – sudden leaps, surprises, they slash the air with their little claws. All of this, they will later need for hunting their prey. Play is after all nothing but preparation for real life.

Young polar bears simply love playing together. They stand up on their hind legs and start fooling around, stimulating their senses and helping them to develop their reflexes. Two bears at play never hurt each other. They keep their desire to play well into maturity. Of course, only mammals and especially those that typically live in groups are capable of playing. We could generalize by saying that the closer an animal species is to humans, the more it enjoys playing. Humanoid apes such as orangutans, chimpanzees and bonobos have the most developed sense of fun. Pets such as dogs and cats which live in close contact with people also like to play whether it is with another dog or with their human friends.

Playtime

3 [1-3] Polar bear infants playing without fear, close to their mother.
[2] Fox cub games often lead to mock fights in which individuals begin to learn and then defend their place in the hierarchy of the group.
[4] Cheetah cubs spend most of their time playing but very soon they start to learn the rituals of dominance and submission.
[5-6] Jack Russell Terrier pups love to play games with balls and toys.

3 [1-2-3] For these Belgian Malinois pups, any object regardless of its size and shape is a source of fun and a reason to play. Pups from the same litter play and romp around together until they are exhausted. Just like human children, pups often acquire a fetish object with which they play, but which also helps to reassure them.

Photo: These are little Shar-Pei pups, with their typically wrinkled skin, at play. When they grow up the deep skin folds will disappear.

[1] For this baby wild boar, running around is the best pastime.
[2-4] Yellow baboon infants often play games which resemble mating behavior. These mating games serve to determine who is dominant and who is submissive in a group.

[5-7] Cheetah cubs very often play together or with their mother.

[1-2-3] This Gelada baby really looks as if it is dancing to music.

[4] Leaping from branch to branch is a favourite game of all orangutans.

[5-8] This young Barbary macaque monkey is hanging on a rope and having good fun while trying to catch fish or berries floating downstream.

The Panther chameleon is native to Madagascar and also occurs on Reunion Island. From an early stage in its life, this gorgeous animal is capable of adopting almost any color, from chestnut brown, to emerald green to white.

S ome animals, different and yet apparently so similar to us, have always filled man with a deep fascination. People have attempted to investigate and determine their intelligence and to understand their behaviour. We have also used our imagination by transforming them into myths and legends.

Our ancestors made up tales of strange creatures, something between human and monster. Those were stories of mythical creatures, chimeras, dragons and terrifying hydras.

These rather eccentric creatures populate the mythology of ancient Greece and Rome and stories of them can be found in medieval manuscripts. We do not have to go that far back in history though. Creatures with strange behavior, bizarre features and rather abnormal shape can be found in present-day biology books. We are used to the giraffe's long neck, the elephant's large trunk, the anteater's cylindrical head and the wrinkled face of the dugong or manatee, which without doubt was the source of the legend of sirens. These animals are real even though they may seem to be more part of myth and legend than of our reality. The seemingly incomplete appearance of some young animals creates an even more bizarre impression on people. Some look as if they have just stepped out of a cartoon or a Hollywood sci-fi movie.

Let's have a look at another rare phenomenon. Some animals lack skin pigmentation. They are completely white, known as albinos, and are very different from their parents.

The main function of colour in animals is for camouflage. Lack of pigment makes albinos easily recognizable and as a result much more vulnerable. In the wild, predators simply spot them too easily and albinos are very often killed prematurely. That is also the reason why we usually only see them in zoos. Some of them have become true media celebrities, like for example Snow Flake, the only albino gorilla kept in Barcelona zoo,

Bizarre babies

which you might already have heard of. If you visited the San Diego zoo in the late 1980's you may have seen Goolara, an albino koala bear with a pink nose and snowy coat, thought to be the only example of an albino koala bear. The Pretoria zoo in the Republic of South Africa owns Archie, an albino penguin.

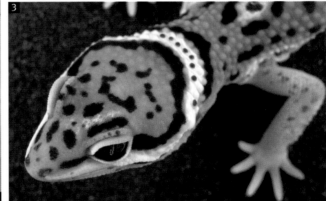

[1-2] A baby red-tailed rat snake can wolf down a whole family of mice.

[3-4] The appearance of a new born Leopard gecko lizard differs substantially from its parents. It is covered with dark-colored dots on yellow skin which gradually disappear and are replaced by speckled patterns on the skin of an adult animal.

[5] The Bearded dragon is a very easy-going reptile which does not object in the least to being moved and handled.
[6] Thanks to suckers on all four legs, the Red-eyed tree frog (*agalychnis callidryas*) has the ability to move vertically on smooth surfaces such as glass.
[7] Most of the time, the baby Moorish gecko clings to its mother's head

[1-2] A baby King Penguin is well protected by its thick fur.

[3] This White-tailed tropic bird is a symbol of Reunion Island. It lays a single egg into hollows and crevices. A tiny fledgling not dissimilar to a fluffy ball is born after the incubation period of the egg is over.

[4] A nestling Grey heron has a funny little tuft on its head. These ones are standing and waiting in the nest for their parents to return with something to eat.
[5-6] Young blindworms have shiny, near-golden skin.

[1] A Silkie chicken is covered with fluffy down-like feathers which give it a somewhat scruffy appearance.
[2] Chameleon infants can, just like adults, turn and roll their eyes independently in all directions.
[3] The Jackson's chameleon has three tiny horns which are meant to intimidate its potential adversaries.
[4] A recently-born Carolina anole lizard is barely three-quarters of an inch long. A grown animal will not achieve lengths of more than 6 inches.

3 [1-3-6] The Madagascar day gecko is a small lizard which is capable of climbing up even the smoothest of vertical surfaces. This little miracle is possible thanks to the flattened toe pads and suckers on the legs of this gorgeous lizard.

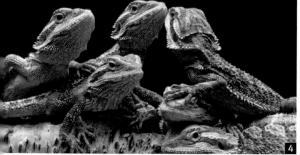

[2-4-5-7] Babies of the Bearded dragon enjoy life in groups and love climbing on branches and plants. These animals are also easy to keep in captivity.

Family life

When feeling threatened, some small fish of the genus Cichlidis (such as *Piscicryptosporidium cichlidis*) hide in their mother's mouth. In case of danger, young lobsters hide under their mother's belly. Only more developed animals, however, can really expect protection from their parents. And it is mostly the female that plays the role of protector to its young.

The role of the father remains limited for most of the time, provided that he does not abandon his impregnated eggs shortly after mating with the female, of course. The mother usually plays her role perfectly well provided that her mother provided her with equally good care. The maternal instinct in a female animal comes to the fore as soon as she starts feeling the presence of her newborns. In mammals, this bond is reinforced by the fact that they lactate, usually over an extended period of time.

In the beginning, a female spends most of the time caring for its young, which are totally dependent on her as far as protection is concerned. Most of all, this applies to newborn ape babies which are carried everywhere by their mother. However, even the babies of some other animals such as antelopes, giraffes and elephants, which are more mature and capable after birth, receive similar attention from their mothers.

The amount of time baby animals spend under their mother's protection differs substantially among animal species. Most rodents leave their mothers immediately after they are weaned. It is not only experience that mothers pass on to their young, it is also love and trust. Experiments have proved that an ape which loses its mother is very likely to choose a surrogate female which will nurse it and provide it with protection. Sooner or later, the day comes when every young animal must become independent. And once again, it is the mother who takes care of this task, sometimes by repelling its baby at times in a somewhat brutal manner.

Protective mothers

The father usually keeps his distance from the young ones. He may wander around but will usually not dare to come close to the female. In wolves, the male always stay clear of the den for the first couple of days. The female would not let him enter the den anyway. Yet male and female wolves do create couples which theoretically last

for the rest of their lives. Inside the den the blind, deaf and hairless pups are nursed by their mother. For several days she does not leave them for a moment and feeds them with her milk. The den is usually situated close to water as she needs to drink a lot to be able to suckle. Out of caution, she may bury some extra food beforehand somewhere nearby. Either way, the male wolf is on the lookout. He usually brings them some of his hunting spoils. First he swallows the food and then regurgitates part of it, pre-digested, in front of the female. Sometimes the female gets help and assistance from other members of the pack. After three weeks, the little wolves are strong enough to open their eyes. With trembling legs, they take their first few steps and begin to play. At the age of two months they gather in front of the den where they are joined by the other wolves of the pack.

At this stage, young and old show as much love and tolerance as possible.

Then, the young wolves start accompanying the adult members of the pack on their hunting trips. They learn how to dismember animals which are brought to them half-dead by their parents and soon they become capable of killing smaller animals on their own. With wintertime approaching (at that time the young wolves are approximately six months old), all members of the pack set out on a journey. Wolves are nomadic hunters capable of covering dozens of miles every day. Such nomadic hunting is typical for wolves.

[1-2-3] For the first time, the wolf cubs leave their den at the age of three weeks. At this age they also begin to play and romp around. [4] There are four to six pups in a litter.

[1] The female wild boar is extremely protective of her young ones and is likely to viciously attack when someone or something appears to pose a threat to her little piglets.

[2] The female giant mouse is so concerned about her babies' safety that she sometimes accidentally swallows them while trying to protect them from predators.

[3] Graylag geese live in groups where females take equal responsibility for, and care of, the young in the community.

[4] The female mouse is a very devoted mother.
[5-6] Graylag geese never leave their fledglings unattended. They are taken care of by both the females and males.

[1] The moorhen leaves its nest only when it needs to get food.
[2] The reproduction rate of Colobus monkeys is very low and mothers therefore need to take great care of their one and only baby.
[3] A female Gentoo penguin is vigorously protecting its single egg as other females who lost theirs are trying to steal it from her.
[4] Female bears love to play with their babies. Usually the Polar bear gives birth to two, less often to one, and even more rarely to three infants in one litter.

4

[1-4] Barbary macaques are social animals. They live in groups which can consist of more than thirty individuals. Females do not leave the groups they are born into whereas males will live with several family groups in their lifetime. Groups are formed by adults (older than five years), sub-adults (3-5 years), young (2-4 years old) males and females and babies (up to 2 years old). The youngest are attended to by all the members of the group. Males in particular spend lots of time with them. They often carry them around and do not stop doing so even when the babies get older.

5 | 6

[5-7] A troop of monkeys is based around the principles of hierarchy which are passed on to the young ones from their mothers. Throughout their lives, young females remain subordinate to their mothers while young males only stay with their mothers until they are six. When relocating, each animal knows where its place within the group is: young males lead, followed by females with infants and the young adult males. The tail of the procession is made up of young males.

7

[1] A baby giraffe is protected not only by its mother
but also by all the other females in the group.
[2] Female elephants are highly devoted mothers.
They watch over their babies for a period of over four years.

2

[1] The Steamer duck is named after its habit of thrashing its wings against the water's surface like a paddle-wheel steamboat. Females often do this in order to protect their fledglings.
[2] The lioness is very attentive to her cubs until the time they get weaned. At that moment, her attitude changes dramatically and sometimes she will even attack them in order to drive them away from her.
[3] After giving birth, the female fox stays in her den for two weeks and feeds her cubs. Even much later she remains a loyal and devoted mother.

[4] Everywhere they go, female hippopotamuses protect their young. They become even more alert whenever they are on dry land where the danger of predatory attacks becomes much higher than in water.

[5-6] African wild dogs are very well organised within their pack. Team spirit is important for these animals: without hesitation, the mothers share their spoils with their pups. They regurgitate partly-digested food for their young ones.

A polar bear cub will grow up to be the largest predator in the Arctic, the true king of the ice. Cubs are born utterly helpless, however, and for long months they remain dependent on their mothers. In early autumn, the pregnant mother withdraws into a shelter which she has dug some 6 to 10 feet under the snow.

And there, deep down under the snow, the female polar bear spends her period of gestation. Despite popular belief, polar bears do not hibernate, even though a pregnant mother goes into dormancy and later gives birth to her young while the male sets out on a journey southwards. Before this however, she must build up a mass of fat tissue which enables her to survive the long, rough winter without food. In around mid-December, she gives birth to two (occasionally one) baby, which she will lavish with extraordinary care and attention. She feeds them with her highly nutritious milk, thanks to which they grow rapidly. Her energy supplies allow her to stay with them at all

In the first days of spring, the female bear and her young leave their cave. Before a baby bear grows strong enough to go on the ice, it stays very close to its mother. To encourage it, she almost constantly licks her baby.

times. When they reach seven weeks, young polar bears learn to crawl and walk on all fours. Later in life, they become resourceful swimmers and excellent divers. Water is their preferred environment, however they are able to move at surprisingly high speed over land as well. They can also slide over ice very efficiently. After some time, the polar bear allows her cubs to go outside the winter cave. From that moment on, they begin to have lessons in how to live and survive in the hostile environment of ice and snow. At first, the small group of mother and cubs always returns to the den for the night. Gradually, though, they begin to explore an ever-increasing area. One day, the mother and her babies do not return, leaving the den for good. This is how their nomadic hunting phase begins. The more limited the territory of the polar bear becomes, the longer their

The polar bear

journeys every year are. This is caused mainly by global warming and by the gradual erosion of icebergs. Hungry polar bears often dare to come close to human settlements, causing unfortunate accidents. Specialised squads have been set up which are authorised to capture and transport the bears by helicopter back to the wild.

[1] Female bears often play gentle games with their little cubs.

[2] The female bear is sitting to make it easier for her baby to suckle.

[3] A baby bear huddling in its mother's lap while she takes a short, relaxing nap.

[4] When a baby bear gets tired, it climbs onto the female's back.
[5] Polar bear cubs just love playing in the snow.
[6] The little ones never stray far from their caring and protective mother.

[1] A female bear supervising her young ones.
[2] Rolling and romping about in the snow are favorites of young polar bears.
[3] A suspicious noise sends the baby bear rushing back to its mother.
[4] Females only reproduce every 3–4 years. Young bears are born after eight months gestation.

[1] At birth, a baby bear weighs one and a half pounds. An adult polar bear may weigh as much as 660 pounds.
[2] The mother and her young often take refuge in holes and caves where they hide from the strong winds.
[3] The female often sleeps through the day. To wake her up, baby bears gently bite her.
[4] A female bear showing her young ones around the territory.
[5] Baby polar bears just love mock fights.
[6] Young bears on an expedition into the surrounding area of the cave. The mother always keeps an eye on them so that they do not stray too far.

[1-4] Young polar bears are always demanding their mother's milk.

[5] The relationship between a mother and her young is one full of love and affection.
[6] Mock fights prepare the young bears for the real fights for territory they will have to face as grown-ups.
[7] A seemingly good-natured bear is in fact an extremely dangerous killing machine especially when accompanied by its young.

A family of crab-eating raccoons spends its life in trees, where the females usually also give birth to their young. The reason for choosing trees as their home is simple – trees offer the best protection against hungry jaguars.

Those babies which are born helpless and immature do, of course, get the most attention from their parents. The task ahead of them is not simple: they must feed and care for their young over a relatively long period of time. Some animal species live what we would call a quiet family life. They grow up together with their mother and father and, if there are any, their siblings.

When the young reach sexual maturity they leave the family to occupy a territory of their own and, of course, to reproduce. Sometimes young animals stay with their parents long enough to see the next litter come into the world. They help their parents to care for their new-born siblings. This gives them many important life lessons. Family life ensures young animals safety, while the adults feed and protect them. The young ones later leave the family unit and become independent.

By their nature, most birds are monogamous creatures. That applies especially in the mating period. Some fathers help with the construction of the nest while others only help to find food for the female and the nestlings. Sooner or later, depending on the species, the young birds reach the stage when they are ready to become independent and do not need their parents any more. Some animal couples stay together for their whole life, though. This is the case with geese and swans, for example. Their young often remain with them even once they are fully capable of an independent existence.

In mammals, the strongest emotional bond existing between animals is that between a mother and her young. In apes, we often find what we would classify as a real family life, very similar to

Perfect families

that of humans. Gibbon mothers and fathers both attend to their children, which leave as late as seven years of age. Their parents stay together. The relationship between a male and a female gibbon lasts a very long time, sometimes throughout their entire lives, and they build their nests with the help of their young.

[1-2-3] Young Mute swans become independent at the age of four and a half months. Until the age of one, however, they live together with their parents. [4] The nest of the Mute swan is usually built on a riverbank where it is guarded and protected by both the male and the female.

[5-6] Goslings of the Orinoco goose do not leave each other until they become old enough to have a family of their own. [7] Just like the young of many other birds of prey, these Eurasian kestrel fledglings are the product of the life-long relationship of their parents.

[1-3] Crab-eating raccoons live in family units where each and every member participates in the task of protecting the whole community against predators.
[2] Female elephants in a group often share the task of protecting the babies.
[4] Cheetahs live in families which consist of several females with young cubs and a single breeding male.

[1-3] Buffalos live in herds of mainly young males and females. In periods of mating, older males come to join the groups.

[5-7] Young buffalos are born after nine months gestation. Buffalos have one litter a year and for the first couple of months, the male stays with the mother and her calf.

[1-3] Ducklings of the same family nestle together.

[4-7] Capybaras, or water hogs, live in groups of twenty which are led by a dominant male. Females have one litter of four to six young per year. Capybaras are the largest known rodents in the world.

259

The lioness is the dominant figure in the family life of lions. They hunt, as well as looking after and protecting their cubs. And yet it is the male who always gets the first bite of the prey, females and cubs only allowed to eat after the males are full.

Half an hour is enough for a zebra to give birth to a baby, while the newborn animal needs no more than twenty minutes and several attempts to get up onto its trembling legs. After two hours it is capable of following its mother. The whole family is present – the male usually watching the scene from a distance.

Then, for three or four days, the mother keeps all other members of the herd at a distance until her newborn learns to recognise her. The female zebra may eventually allow older siblings to clean and lick the newborn baby. This task is then regularly performed by the attentive and caring male. He keeps his eye on the foal and brings it back to the group if it strays too far away or falls asleep the herd. During the first few months, the young zebra follows its mother everywhere she goes. In dry periods, the mother sometimes withdraws to find water which she needs more than ever while lactating. At such a time, she leaves her baby alone, exposed to danger. Lions are always lurking nearby. Luckily, the herd is usually ready to defend its members. When the young as well as the adult animals rest, one zebra stays awake and, in the event of danger, makes loud sounds to alarm the rest of the group. The young can easily find their mothers by smell or by the unique pattern of black and white stripes. This pattern is also what helps to identify different kinds of zebra. There are in fact three: the Cape mountain zebra, the Grevy's zebra and the Burchell's zebra (more often referred to as the Plain zebra).

A baby zebra, well surrounded

When a zebra wants to show its baby that the time to be weaned has come, it drives it gently away and if that does not work, she starts biting its rump. Once she has stopped feeding it, the female still tends to provide the young animal with care and attention for many more months.

[1] Young zebras are a favorite prey of lions.
[2] A zebra is born with a specific hair pattern which remains the same for its whole life. It is only the hue of this pattern that changes.
[3] Baby zebras are nursed by their mothers over a period of six to seven months.
[4] Stripes can be found everywhere on a zebra's body, the mane being no exception.
[5-6] Until they are two years old, young zebras stay with their family of one adult male and one or two females.

[1-2] The baby zebra never strays too far from its mother.
[3] Zebras live in groups which move over great distances in the savannah.
[4] Isolated young individuals usually soon become a target for predators.

[5] Even after being weaned, young zebras stay close to their mothers.
[6] By imitating the mother, a baby zebra learns to tell the good, tasty grass from the bad.
[7] Zebras very seldom lay down. They do it only when they want to roll in the dust to rid themselves of parasites.

[1] Thanks to its superb camouflage, this little zebra is very well hidden in the tall grass.
[2] Young zebras stay together until they are two years old.
[3] Just like many other mammal species, a mother and her young recognize each other by their scent.

[4] A baby zebra's hair is sometimes of a different hue to that of its mother. With age, it becomes the same, though.
[5-6] Quite often we can see signs of deep affection among zebras, especially between a mother and her baby.

Sometimes a jackal pup accidentally returns to the wrong den. It is usually accepted by its inhabitants and cared for. When African wild dog pups lose their parents, mostly as a result of a predatory attack, other members of the pack feed them and take turns in nursing them.

This solidarity usually stems from life in a social group, though we can also sometimes observe this type of behaviour in animals which bring up their young alone. Some communities willingly protect the young ones. In case of danger, the musk oxen make a protective circle around their young. Sometimes, an individual male or female helps a mother in need with her young. This is what we could call godparenthood. Wolves and wild dogs send one or more animals to watch the group's young while the rest of the pack goes hunting.

At birth, "godparents" assist whales or dolphins to swim to the surface to breathe. When an ape gets too tired to carry its baby any further, it is the godfather or godmother that takes care of it. Lionesses have often been observed nursing cubs of other females. And when a lioness goes hunting, it is her sister, cousin or even a non-related female that stays with the cubs.

There is a great deal of solidarity among female elephants. When one of them gives birth to a baby, the others stay with her for at least two days until the little one is capable of walking and running. Life in a community offers other forms of help too. Several adult animals will watch over a number of young ones which gather in a sort of nursery while the parents are busy securing food or water. When American elks leave in search of

Godmothers and nurseries

food, the young ones stay huddled closely together, waiting under the supervision of other members of the group. The same strategy is used by baby Emperor penguins. They, too, gather their offspring in nurseries within their colonies. It is not unusual to see one whole generation of young penguins in there.

[1] The time to nest has come. These Cape gannets are gathering.
[2] Within the protection of these enormous nurseries, blue-eyed cormorants lay 2–3 blue eggs. Parents then take it in turns to sit on them.
[3] The Magellanic penguins keep their young in these huge nurseries. Parents take it in turns to search for food for their offspring.

[4] In order to ensure their safety, Rockhopper penguins create groups with a number of babies.
[5] Female common shags nest in huge colonies.
[6] When Magellanic penguins grow older, their colony shifts towards the sea front where the baby penguins can start taking their first fishing lessons.

[1-2] Orinoco geese bring up their goslings in nurseries, the females taking turns in caring for the babies.
[3-4] Baby ostriches are never alone: they all are brought up together in small groups which are protected by watchful females.

[5] [6]

[5] Little red-fronted lemurs are watched by adults in nurseries which are built in the treetops.
[6] Young colobus monkeys are often brought up with the help of an aunt or even a grandmother.
[7] Young wild boars are never left unattended in the wild: they live in groups supervised by caring females.

[7]

The absence of family life is a feature of most lower animal species. In most insects, reptiles, fish and amphibians, the male and female part immediately after fertilization of their eggs. As soon as the female lays its eggs, it usually loses all interest in their fate.

The offspring are then left at the mercy of the environment and its predators. Most of them die. Fortunately, these animals lay enormous numbers of eggs which give some of the young a fair chance of survival. Mothers often lay their eggs in places which provide the young with food as soon as they have hatched. That is certainly the case for most insect species. Many species also hide their eggs before they abandon them.

Unlike mammals and birds, these babies must be able to cope on their own and live and learn without any guidance. Fish spread out their eggs in the water. The larvae, minute at birth, risk being eaten by their own parents. There are numerous exceptions though. The stickleback spreads the impregnated eggs by means of its sea wings, which ensures they do not go mouldy. The young then stay with their father for some time.

The male seahorse also cares for its eggs until the young have hatched. He keeps the eggs in a type of incubation pouch. They are put there by the female.

Most reptiles do not care in the least for their young. Fortunately enough for them, they have a supply of nutritious material in the form of the yolk. This allows the embryo to grow and survive. Turtles swim thousands of miles in order to lay

Abandoned eggs

their eggs in the best place possible. Immediately after their task is fulfilled, they abandon their eggs in the sand.

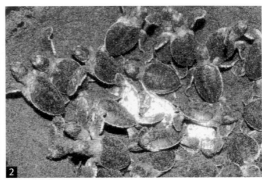

[1-8] Just like all other species of its kind, the green sea turtle does not care for its eggs. After they hatch, the young set out on an extremely dangerous trip to the sea. The beaches are swarming with waiting predators and the only chance the tiny helpless turtles have is to be as quick as possible and to get as far into the sea as they can. If successful, they stay there for some time before returning to dry land. The young turtles use up stored energy supplies which allow them to survive without food for a couple of weeks.

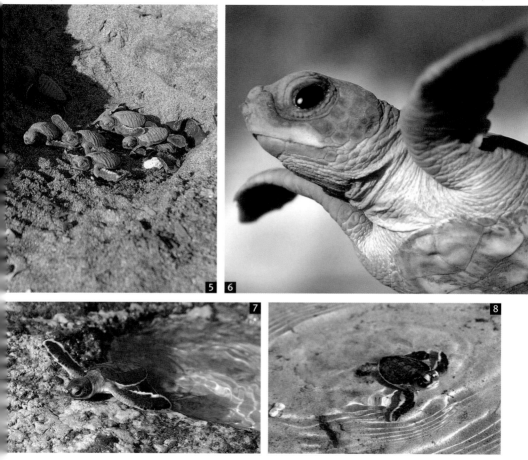

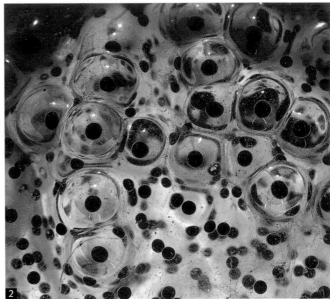

[1] Frogs are completely indifferent to the eggs they lay. The tadpoles survive only thanks to energy supplies, in the form of the yolk, stored in their tiny bodies.
[2] The eggs of the common frog are laid in large clusters in safe waters.
[3] The Ring-necked snake lays and abandons its eggs in the wild, more often than not near water.

[4] The common frog lays an unbelievable number of eggs: between 1,500 and 4,000, usually in backwaters. The tadpoles hatch after two to three weeks. Their growth and development takes two to three months and then they metamorphose into their fully developed form.

Everyday
life

Whether they have one pair of teats, like apes or elephants, or two or three pairs like cows or even five to seven pair like sows, all female mammals feed their young with their own milk.

That applies to those that are helpless and must stay hidden in a den for some time as well as to those baby animals that are almost immediately capable of standing up on all fours alongside their mother.

The first thing those helpless baby animals, that cannot stand, do after they are born is to find their way to their mother's precious teats. Those babies that can get up, suckle on their mother's teats while standing or in a slight crouch. Mothers often help them by pushing them towards the right place. This moment is of vital importance, especially in the first few days. A close bond is created between a mother and her baby. They get to know each other, and their scents, and establish a deep affection with each other. The period of lactation differs between species – a baby elephant lives off its mother's milk until four years of age while the Tenrec, a small insect-eater, native to the island of Madagascar, gets weaned after a mere week of suckling. The young are therefore totally dependent on their mothers, while the fathers' responsibilities remain mostly limited.

A mother's milk is very rich and nourishing, even though its content and nutritional value differs between species. In any case, it is the best food for their early growth and development and ensures a young animal will grow quickly, until it is weaned by its mother. In the beginning, babies drink whenever they feel the urge, until their appetite is satisfied. Then the frequency of feedings decreases and the animals gradually switch from milk to solid food. Very often, animals

Feeding baby mammals

continue to suckle even after they have started eating normal food.

In any case, in all mammals the day comes when the baby becomes independent - which in most cases also means parting with the parents. This moment is often identical to the moment an infant is weaned.

[1-3] A short-haired dachshund bitch can have as many as ten pups in one litter.
[2] This cute little Malinois pup is demanding a drink of milk from its mother, who has been weakened by intense feeding.

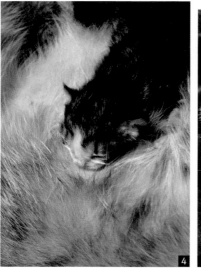

[4-5] Immediately after birth, baby kittens instinctively head for the teats for their first drink of milk. They are solely led by their instincts.
[6] From the very first day, Shar-pei dogs fight for a place at the teats.

[1] This baby domesticated Aurochs is being nursed by its mother, just like its wild ancestors were, thousands of years ago.

[2-3 and right] Shortly after birth, a baby Gerenuk looks almost identical to the adult with its typically long neck and legs which also give it the nickname, the Giraffe Antelope. While feeding its baby, the mother is always standing on guard.

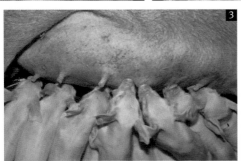

[1] The wild sow lactates for a period of five months.
[2] A lioness nursing her cubs outside her group.
[3] To improve the breeding ability of pigs, people have tried to identify those females that are capable of having the highest number of piglets in one litter.

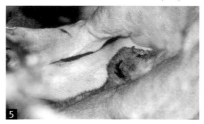

[4] When a lion cub grows bigger, it is nursed within a group. When fighting for places at the lioness's teats, it becomes clear which the stronger and weaker are.

[5] After being born, it takes a lion cub no more than a couple of minutes to find its mother's teats.

[6] A baby elephant drinks with its trunk pointing upwards.

[7] A near-adult zebra still continues suckling until the moment its mother drives it away for good.

[1] The stretching exercises of an orangutan mother do not prevent her baby from having a sip of milk.
[2-3] A newborn Barbary macaque monkey spends long hours in its mother's lap, feeding comfortably.

[4] When a Bontebok antelope grows larger it must go down on its knees in order to be able to drink.
[5] A camel's milk is very rich in water which allows the young to survive without any kind of water source.
[6] When nursing, the cougar always leaves its group to find a quite place in the shade.

[1-2] Even though seal pups are not slaughtered in front of their nursing mothers any more, seal hunts continue to take place. As a result, thousands of these animals are killed every year during legal hunts.
[3] When a sea elephant baby wants to inform its mother that it is hungry, it starts emitting throaty screams not dissimilar to burping.

[4] Male sea elephants live surrounded by their females in a sort of harem which can consist of as many as ten females. Trying to get close to a lactating female is a highly dangerous activity. The males are always nearby and ready to attack.

The shape and color of the open beaks of Great tit fledglings is a strong signal for the parents that it is high time they fed their hungry young ones.

Some birds, such as ducks and small water birds, are able to feed themselves very soon after they hatch. They are referred to as precocial birds. Others come into the world helpless and naked, and must be fed by one of their parents until they grow strong enough to survive on their own. These are called altricial species.

The parents of young which belong to the latter group must collect solid food such as insects, worms and fishes. Their nestlings cry out, standing up on their legs and opening their beaks wide so as not to be ignored at feeding time. By doing this they in fact trigger the desired pattern of behaviour in their parents. Pigeons and doves feed their young with a fatty liquid, similar to the milk of mammals, which is produced by the bird's crop.

Some bird species, such as pigeons and hens, are vegetarians and live mainly on seeds. Their strong, hard beaks enable small parrots to crack even the hardest of seeds. Blackbirds and thrushes love berries, while the hummingbird feeds on nectar which it licks out of flowers with its slender beak and long, brush-shaped tongue. Other birds are insectivores. A swallow will dive into a swarm of flies with its beak wide open and come out with a small ball of insects which it then feeds to its hungry fledglings. Other bird species hunt for fish: wading birds, such as the Greater flamingo, combs with its large beak through sand, while other birds of prey can catch a fish in full flight by diving head-first into water. Carnivorous birds, mainly birds of prey, feed their fledglings on other birds, small rodents or even rabbits.

In late summer, when certain insects, berries and

How to feed a fledgling

fruit become sparse in the wild, some birds adapt their diet to the new conditions. But other bird species are unable to adapt, and must migrate elsewhere so as to be able to find food. Prior to the start of their journey, they build up supplies in the form of hypodermic fatty tissue and as a result their weight can as much as double.

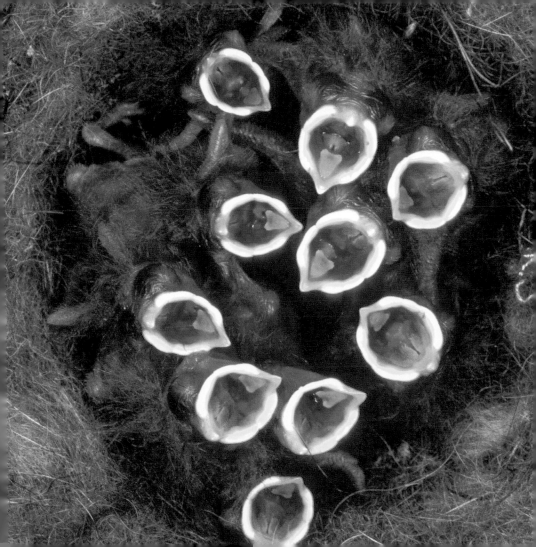

[1] A Marabou stork feeding on cadavers. Dead animals are the main constituent of their diet.
[2] The Royal eagle hunts for small birds, rodents and reptiles, which it kills to feed its young.
[3] To catch enough fish for its young nestlings as well as for itself, the great crested grebe dives to kill in ponds and lakes.

[4-7] Young Blue tits are eager for flies, butterflies, worms and caterpillars. Females and males take it in turns to search for food. They return with the prey still alive in their beaks.

3

[1-2] A wren coming back to its fledglings with some fresh spiders and live insects.

[3] The short-toed eagle lives mainly on a diet of snakes. The mother also feeds them to her young.

[4-5] The nest of the Golden oriole is spherical, usually hanging at the end of a horizontal branch. For safety reasons, it is built as far from the trunk as possible, which ensures the nestlings are safe from climbing predators such as weasels. The fledglings live off a diet consisting of insects and berries.

[6] A young blue tit opens its colorful beak in order to be fed by its mother.

[1] In order to get enough food for its young, the Barn swallow is always flying back and forth between its nest and hunting territory.
[2] A snowy owl bringing small rodents for its hungry offspring.

[1-2] The Eurasian jays build their nests in pairs. As construction material, they mainly use fine roots. The nest is usually situated somewhere between 6 and a half and 16 feet above the ground. The fledglings are fed with acorns, berries and also lizards.

[3-4] The female [3] together with the male [4] Red-backed shrike are feeding their young. Due to the fact that it mates sporadically, and usually has fewer fledglings than other birds, the Red-backed shrike is an endangered species.

[5-9] A barn swallow feeding its fledglings may remind you of a ballet dancer. The bird balances on the spot so as to be able to place insects into each babies' beak.

[1] A female Northern gannet is gutting a fish caught for its young.
[2-3 and right] Baby King Penguins live exclusively on fish usually caught by their parents in the open sea, often many miles away from the nest.

The main goal of most wild animals is to find enough food to survive. Very young mammals which are cared for by their mothers over longer or shorter periods of time must gradually learn how to get along on their own.

As their milk teeth develop, they switch slowly from milk to solid food. This is the case with most insectivores, herbivores and carnivores.

From their mothers, young animals learn how to live and survive on their own. And they learn very well indeed: a baby ape skilfully stealing fruit and leaves from its mother is a common sight in ape families. The baby clings to its mother and tries out different types of food to see which have the best flavour. A cheetah cub, on the other hand, likes to play around with dead animals previously hunted and killed by its mother. It will soon become as great a meat eater as its parents. Herbivores usually grow very strong incisor teeth and flat molars which enable them to pluck, chew and grind plants that are on their daily menu. Herbivores nibble – just as rodents such as rabbits, mice or squirrels do – or they graze like a sheep or horse.

Carnivores, on the other hand, have very mighty canine teeth and sharp molars which they use to tear off pieces of meat from dead bodies and grind bones. Many, such as lions and tigers, will not refuse dead animals, the favorite diet of hyenas and jackals. In the company of adults, young animals take part in the daily carnage. Bats hunt for insects, just as moles, anteaters and pangolins do. Some mammals hunt in water: polar bears hunt for ducks, while otters mostly catch fish which they then eat on a riverbank or on

What mammals eat

rocks. And because there are different tastes, there are also animals which prefer one particular food either because they choose to because of its flavour or simply because they have no other option: koala bears eat mainly eucalyptus leaves and pandas, once they have passed six months, feed exclusively on juicy bamboo shoots.

[1] On the island of Madagascar, the red-fronted Brown lemur feeds on leaves and tree bark.
[3] A baby baboon collects fruit, leaves, small insects and worms. Later, it will even eat the flesh of larger mammals such as antelopes.

[2-4] Giraffes live off the leaves which grow on tall trees,
preferably thorny ones such as those found on acacia trees.

3 [1-3] Even though this young mouflon, at this stage of its life still without its characteristic horns, has not yet been weaned, it is already learning how and on what to graze.
[2] Horses mainly eat grass. A mare is showing its foal how to avoid poisonous plants such as crowfoot.

[4] A she-wolf, having been encouraged by her pups, is regurgitating pre-digested food.

[5] This young coyote is very hungry and so is licking its mother. This encourages her feed him.

[6] A fox cub is waiting for its mother to regurgitate food for it.

[1] The laughing hyena lives off carrion. It eats both fresh and rotting meat.
[2] Zebras mainly live off grass, only very rarely eating the leaves from trees.

Some animals spend lots of time sleeping, especially newborns. They spend their first few days huddled next to the mother, waking only to suckle her milk. Just like human babies, they also dream their first dreams. Some scientists have concluded that cats are even able to dream of hunting.

The length of sleep differs substantially between animal species. A rabbit, for example, sleeps very briefly, which is without a doubt caused by the fact that it feels threatened and must therefore stay alert most of the time. Animals in general have to adapt their sleeping patterns to the environment they live in. For instance, predators can sleep for long periods of time – as much as eighteen hours a day. They certainly sleep better and for longer

Sleeping

than their prey can afford to. Some animals, by taking a short nap during the day, are able to remain alert and observant: their main task is to watch over and ensure the safety of their babies, after all. An opossum, with more than twenty hours of sleep, is the record holder, while a shark never sleeps a wink in its life. Some animals sleep during the day while others sleep at night. Owls, beavers, bats, rabbits, and squirrels all become active at sundown, after a whole day of rest. Animals go hunting to satisfy not only their needs but also those of their young. Sometimes the young accompany them on their night hunting parties, as is common in bats, for example.

For some animal species, such as the hedgehog, squirrel, brown bear or bat, the first frosts in autumn mean the beginning of a long sleep. Initially they eat as much food as possible and then they withdraw into their winter dens which are covered with grass, leaves and sometimes even hair. There they hibernate.

They remain there in a state of deep sleep, the body's rhythm slowing down to a bare minimum. They regularly wake up for a few of hours, leave their shelters to stretch, drink and eat and then return to sleep again. Some animals even give birth to their babies during this period. Most reptiles and amphibians hibernate too. As soon as it gets warm, adults as well as young animals, their bodies weakened and lean after a long period of deep sleep, begin returning to life again.

[1-2] A baby reindeer takes a nap while its parents watch over it. [3] Just like most other cold-blooded animals, young alligators enjoy sleeping in the sun.

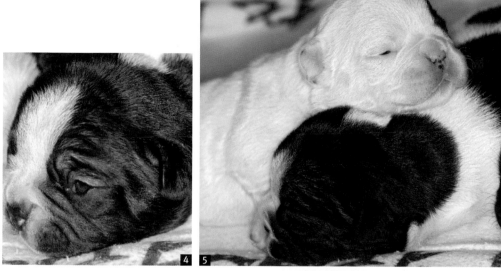

[4-5-6] These French bulldog puppies, just a few days old, sometimes sleep through three quarters of the day.

[1-2-3] In the heat of the midday sun, lions usually take shelter and rest under acacia trees. They begin to hunt only after the sun goes down.

[4] A cub takes a rest on its mother's belly.

[1] Lion cubs, huddled together on their mother's stomach, await the adults waking up.
[2] A long yawn and here he goes, a baby albino lion is waking up!
[3] Together with her cubs, this lioness is enjoying the cooling shade of a bush. A great place to unwind, isn't it.
[4] A fawn is ready to curl up into a fetal position and take a short nap.

[5-6] During the day, Bengal tigers rest. They sprawl around lazily, only becoming active after sunset.
[7] An exhausted cheetah falls asleep after having been hunting with its mother.

[1] A young Barbary macaque relaxes on its sleeping mother.
[2] Hippopotamuses retire to dry land to sleep.

A lion roars in front of its cub. In this way, the cub learns how to make its voice heard. By doing so, it reaffirms its position as the dominant male of the group.

The language of animals, or to put it in other words, the means animals employ to communicate, has always been a mystery. Ethnologists, that is, scientists who specialise in the study of animal behavior, have made great progress, undertaking hundreds of hours of observation and analysis. From the moment they are born, animals have numerous ways of expressing how they feel.

Animals can also express what position they occupy in the world as well as their social standing within the hierarchy of a group. Animals use various means of communication: scent, colour, sound, posture, mimic and other gestures. They also learn to mark their territory in different ways: visually, through sound or scent. By means of different patterns of behavior, adult animals can warn their young about various types of danger or show them where to search for food. Young animals must, in turn, be able to let their parents know that they are hungry or that they are afraid of something.

There are also specific relations between a mother and her baby which they need to learn to recognise and understand as circumstances change. Over the course of the first few hours of an animal's life, it must learn to recognise its mother and store this crucial piece of information in its memory. It can be the shape of her body, the sound of her breathing or her scent. A goat, for example, can recognize her baby only provided that she learns and memorises its scent. She learns it by licking and smelling her newborn immediately after birth. Five minutes are enough for her to have learned to recognize

Communication,
or the language of animals

her baby and thus avoid rejecting it by accident later on.

Myna birds, like parrots, are capable of imitating the human voice. These animals only imitate and

[1] The giraffe's long neck prevents it from making any sounds and the only way it can communicate with its babies is through gentle gestures.

repeat the sounds without understanding them, of course. Birds, frogs and many kinds of reptiles make various sounds which at the same time serve as social signals. Animals have around thirty-five different signals in their repertoire which serve to warn against danger, to call a relative or to express their emotions. It is, though, a far cry from the complexity of human language: articulate, complicated and inventive as it is. There are exceptions. Research into chimpanzee communication has produced some surprising results. The level of communication between parent and infant is often surprisingly effective. Initially simple and straightforward, it gradually becomes more ingenious and complex. Even before a bird has hatched out of its egg, it learns to distinguish the voice of its parents from other background noise. Whenever it hears the voice of its young, the crocodile immediately comes to the rescue. Parents usually know how to let their young ones know, clearly and quickly, that there is danger of some sort nearby. Some can even produce different signals depending on the type of danger present. The Californian squirrel makes one particular sound when it notices a bird of prey and another when it sees a snake approaching.

Young animals learn by imitating what they see. A nestling becomes familiar with birdsong long before it can sing itself. A young nightingale that has lost its parents and only hears the song of a warbler will soon become able to imitate its song as opposed to the nightingale's typical song. It is important to realize that there are not only sounds which we hear and identify, such as barking, mooing or whinnying, but also sounds we cannot hear: for example the sounds made by bats and rodents which communicate using ultrasound.

[2] Thanks to their enormous ears, bats are capable of recognising ultrasound signals made by other bats.
[3] The word "magpie" originally comes from the French, meaning "chatterbox."
[4] Magellanic penguins whistle whenever they want to attract the attention of their parents.
[5] Bonobos are apes which communicate through facial expression. These are very close to human facial expressions, though they cannot speak.

[1-3] Lions often lick each other: though this is a gesture of submission rather than an expression of tenderness.
[2] A lioness roars to drive her cub away because she does not feel like feeding it at this moment.

[4] A cub has succeeded in carefully approaching the dominant male and now it is gently touching his muzzle in order to express submission to him.
[5] A young lion quickly learns how to utilise its roar to reaffirm its position within the hierarchy of the group.

3 [1] When a lion cub paws bark, it does so in order to leave its scent there. This is one of the many ways lions mark their territory.
[2] The aggressive growling of the tiger always comes as a sign of imminent attack.
[3] By licking her muzzle, a young, hungry jackal is in fact asking its mother to feed it.

[4] The bellow of the stag is designed to court and attract young females, at the same time deterring other males.

[1-2-3] It is enough to show a female of the Blue jay bird a piece of red cloth, the color of which is identical to its fledglings' mouth, and she will react by putting food on it.
[4] Chickens which lose their mother and are left close to an object, animal or human will follow it and behave as if it was their mother.

[5] Baboons make lots of gestures with their hands, as if speaking in their own sign language.
[6] For the macaque, mutual grooming for bugs is a very important communication ritual.
[7] The female elephant trumpets before charging, to deter those who may want to harm her babies.

[1-2-3] King Penguins communicate mainly through sound. A female can recognise her baby's voice among thousands of other penguins.

[4-6] Young manatee communicates with its mother using continual chirps and squeaks.
[5] Young dolphins learn to make around a dozen different sounds, including whistling, rattling and clicking.

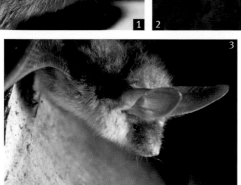

[1-4] European bat species such as the Common bat [1], the Bechstein's bat [2-3] and the Madagascan flying fox [4] communicate through sounds inaudible to the human ear.

[5] One day it will be bellowing in the rutting season, but at the moment this young White-tailed deer can only squeal.
[6] The delicate gestures of a female orangutan are very similar to human gestures.
[7] A wolf cub is licking its mother's muzzle, which encourages her to regurgitate food for her young one.

347

When they reach approximately two and a half years of age, young panthers leave their mothers to start lives of their own. After a long period of training and education, they become very solitary animals and great hunters.

Over the course of these two years, three or four cubs from the same litter remain in basically the same place they were born, because panthers are quite conservative, rarely changing territory. In areas rich in game, the territories are smaller than in areas with a shortage of prey. Male territories are generally speaking larger than those of females, with which they often overlap. Nevertheless, the females never interfere with the territories of the males. In order to mark and confirm its territory, the male panther leaves its scent on vegetation, as well as leaving paw prints on the bark of trees or on stones. When doing so, the male usually makes sounds similar to rough coughing. Panthers, like other felines, are very expressive. For example, the way a panther holds its tail can mean various things. Panthers use a broad range of sounds and expressions and teach their cubs how to use them. When a panther wants to attract its cubs' attention, it starts making short, abrupt sounds. A short growl is a clear sign of recognition, however if it is accompanied by a snuffle it usually means that the panther is going to attack. Before setting out to hunt, panthers first make a short, light coughing sound, while the point at which an attack is imminent, the animal starts roaring. When they reach their third month, the cubs begin to accompany their parents on hunting trips. A few weeks later, they are able to catch prey on their own as well as, to a certain extent, imitating their mother's sounds. By her side, they

The language of panthers

learn to be patient and cunning.

An adult panther is a master of camouflage and concealment, which means it is never where you would expect it to be. Panthers teach their cubs the art of avoiding traps by taking detours, and they also train them how to reach their desired goal at any price.

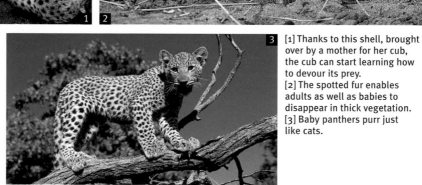

[1] Thanks to this shell, brought over by a mother for her cub, the cub can start learning how to devour its prey.
[2] The spotted fur enables adults as well as babies to disappear in thick vegetation.
[3] Baby panthers purr just like cats.

[4] Trees are the panther's watchtowers. They also relax there. They often take their prey up into the trees. A tree is a place where they can eat undisturbed by hyenas and other carnivores.

[1] Through games panthers learn patience. Patience is, after all, one of their dominant features.
[2] When baby panthers climb trees, they miaow and make whistling sounds. These sounds are thought to express the satisfaction that comes with achievement.

Whenever wild rabbits leave
their den, they firstly wash
their fur thoroughly.

Animal parents spend lots of time washing their babies. Usually, they do it thoroughly and systematically because good hygiene helps to keep their offspring in good health. For birds as well as for mammals, washing is a necessity: it helps to keep fur or feathers nice and clean, helps to rid animals of parasites and last but not least, washing helps to create important bonds between adult animals and their young.

baby and she herself absorbs its scent, which allows them to recognise each other from that moment on, even in a large group of other animals of their kind.

Washing will later become a solitary activity, except for the time of mating when females lick males and vice versa. It can, though less often, also fulfil a social function: old and young, relatives or strangers within a group, some animals spend lots of time picking bugs from the fur of others. This activity is typical for monkeys and apes, though wolves, for example, also sometimes do it as an aspect of social behavior within the pack.

Water, dust and mud are the main means of maintaining hygiene in animals. A hippopotamus, like an otter, washes itself in water, whereas birds make do with puddles. Some mammals, such as elephants or bears, rub their skin or fur against tree trunks to rid themselves of annoying parasites. Felines usually have long tongues, with

Washing is often the first form of contact between a young animal and its mother: the very moment it is born, the mother licks her baby to clean and dry it. She continues doing this until it grows old enough to do it on its own. The initial washing is essential to make the blood of a newborn circulate properly and to make it breathe regularly, and it is often the mother's tongue which shows her baby the way to her teats. Licking is also important for the process of recognition. The mother leaves her scent on the

Washing and being washed

specially shaped papilla which allow them to clean their bodies with surprising efficiency. The fur of tigers and panthers has a velvety appearance. The lion, though, is exceptional in this aspect: old dirty hair in its mane is apparently not a reason to worry. The lioness, on the other hand, washes her cubs regularly and diligently.

[1-4] Japanese macaques spend a lot of time in mutual delousing. Females help to rid their babies of all sorts of troublesome bugs and lice. The young ones often delouse each other as well as their mothers or other adults.

[5] With great care and attention, a female baboon is delousing her baby.
[6] A kitten wetting its paw so that it can wash those parts of its body which cannot be cleaned directly by the tongue.
[7] Here a female cat is licking her kitten's fur to keep it clean.

[1-2] Bengal tiger cubs have learned from their mother how to clean their paws but they are also instructed how to keep their claws sharp and in good condition. Those are their weapons of survival after all.

[3] Young Bengal tigers often clean adult members of their family group. This is a clear sign of submission towards the adult animals.

[4] A lioness licks her cub. When the lion cubs grow older,
they will provide this service to one another.

1

[1] Mud-bathing helps this baby elephant get rid of parasites.
[2] With great care and tenderness this Gerenuk cleans her young one.

The trunk is a useful tool:
elephants use it as a shower,
to wet and dust their bodies.

E lephants cannot survive without water. The daily amount of water used by an individual animal is approximately 25 gallons. Not only does an elephant need to drink an enormous amount of water to survive, it also needs to be able to bathe and immerse its huge body in water. Members of a group, both young and old, must therefore spend some part of every day by a pond, lake or river. These water reservoirs often become meeting points for different herds of elephants.

time playing, wash time is at the top of its list of daily routines.

As elephants drink, they shower their heads and bodies, splashing happily, and spraying the vital liquid all over themselves, eventually immersing themselves in water or lying down in a riverbed with only their trunk above the water's surface. For baby elephants these are moments of pure joy: splashing, pushing one another, rolling and spraying water on their friends. All this usually takes place under the supervision of the mothers or aunts who sometimes step in to cool their great enthusiasm. If there is mud around, it only adds to the elephants' joy. Baby elephants collect it in their trunks and throw it all over their bodies. Then they lie down in mud pools and roll around until every square inch of their bodies is covered in it. From grey they swiftly become a glossy black. When all members of the

The oldest female in the group always remembers where these vitally important, though scarce, locations are, passing this life-saving know-

Elephant bathing and water games

ledge on to future generations. In a forest, elephants drink whenever they find themselves in marshland. In the open spaces of the savannah they often wash in the middle of the day or shortly before sundown. For a baby elephant that spends lots of its

herd are refreshed, the group has to continue their journey. Though with some reluctance, the babies leave with them. Later in the day, exhausted, the young elephants lie down in the shade of a tree and doze off.

[1-4] In the vast open spaces of the African savannah, elephants often cover immense distances. However they always plan stops at points which provide water for washing and refreshment. If they reach a place which seems to have dried out on the surface, adults dig a hole in the ground so as to get at the underground water. This technique usually proves successful.

[5-6] Baby elephants, exposed to the heat and fierce sunshine, need to drink several hundred litres of water every day.
[7] In South Africa, elephants often come to the coast to wash and cool down.

[1-3] When deciding whether or not to stay in an area, a female elephant always takes into consideration its baby's daily requirement of water and fresh grass.

[4] Elephants do not hesitate when a river needs to be crossed.
They either swim or, as in this picture, safely wade across.

[1-7] Baby elephants simply adore the water and if they could, they would stay there for hours on end, always under the supervision of their mothers of course.

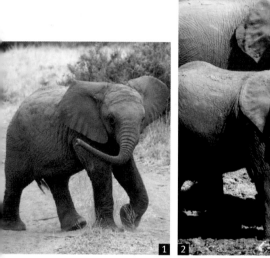

[1-2] After a bath, elephants often cover their bodies with a fine dust.

[3] Taking into consideration the needs of their young, mothers always search for grassy areas near water.

[4-7] Elephants and their young often cover great distances, and during their journeys they take numerous refreshment stops. During this time it is not unusual to see both hunter and prey side by side. This is called the water truce.

371

[1-6] A female elephant is training its baby in the art of finding water. She will also show it how to extract water from certain plant species such as the spongy trunks of baobabs which are literally filled with water, or in succulents such as the euphorbia plant and aloes.

In a town,
on a farm

Whatever our opinion on the subject may be, birds are not the only animals living in urban areas. Though less visible, insects, fish and even mammals are also present and active in city parks, on streets, in sewers or in the attics of our houses.

Thanks to the heating systems in houses and to exhaust fumes, cities are warmer than ever before and in places such as rubbish bins there is always enough food to be found.

Trees produce oxygen and, just like roofs and chimneys, they are great places for nests. More than eighty bird species live in the city. Some build their nests there but only about ten bird species reside in urban environments permanently. City heat allows some species to reproduce a considerable time before the warm weather arrives. In parks and gardens, small islands of nature within the concrete jungle, tiny yet complex worlds meet. There they gather and wait for night to fall. For reasons of safety, animals in the city often become nocturnal. Moles, squirrels, weasels,

In the Alsace-Lorraine region of France, just as in other locations across Europe, storks build massive nests on roofs, chimneys and the smoke stacks of abandoned factories.

rabbits and many other animals can be spotted by an attentive observer in a neighbourhood at night. Houses are the domain of house mice which reproduce extremely quickly and efficiently, like the rats which flood the sewers and cellars of some urban areas. It has been estimated that there are as many rats in the city of Paris as there are people. Bats and barn owls, on the other hand, live with their young in attics. Rivers, which often flow quite lazily through cities, are home to numerous fish species though only a few are able to reproduce there. This is due to the sparse river vegetation, something necessary for the survival of their eggs. Occasionally a fox strays into the city in search of food while its cubs wait for her in the nearby nature. Foxes are, however, rarely seen on the streets. Cities and towns often have some

Baby animals in cities

very exotic inhabitants in the realms of fauna and flora. Ailanthus, a tree native to Asia, has adapted to the climate and environment of urban parks and public gardens, having been imported by the Sphinx moth, a butterfly which is naturally hosted by the tree. This imported insect is now the largest nocturnal butterfly in Europe.

[1] Mice are small rodents which live together with humans. They often make their nests in attics and steal food from people's houses and gardens.
[2] Kittiwakes live in high numbers in cities situated by the sea or ocean shore. In winter, the birds migrate deeper inland.
[3] Swifts can often be spotted in downtown areas, as they choose mainly tall buildings for their nests.

[4] The common house martin is a house dweller; abandoned and derelict buildings often swarm with these elegant, agile little birds.
[5] The barn swallow, also known as common swallow, prefers villages to towns.
[6] If a fox gets hungry, it often ventures into towns where it explores the contents of rubbish bins and containers.

1 **2**

3

[1] The magpie can often be seen near human dwellings. Because this animal does not fear humans, it can be easily domesticated.

The carrion crow often drives magpies out of their nests, while magpies steal sparrows' eggs. This is where its reputation as a thief originates.

[2-3-4] The barn owl nests in attics, old belfries and clock-towers.
As a nocturnal animal, it only comes out at night when hunting for mice and other rodents.

[1-4] The cunning weasel knows how to find empty buildings and abandoned attics where it often gives birth to its young. It is a typically nocturnal animal which feeds on diet of small mammals, particularly rodents, though it will make do with birds, insects, and worms, and will also nibble at fruit which it often steals from gardens.

[5] Swallows nestle in rocks and crevices near city houses, very often keeping us company in parks.
[6] The Red-eared terrapin, available in pet stores, very often ends up in city lakes and public parks where people get rid of them.
[7] Mallards live in park ponds, rivers and lakes. People often come with their children to feed these peaceful birds.

The feral pigeon is the most common city dweller among birds. Sadly, pigeons and doves cause extensive damage in urban areas with their guano. There are many species of pigeons, including the wood pigeon, the rock pigeon, the stock pigeon, the hill pigeon, the carrier pigeon, and the Eurasian or white-collared pigeon.

Kittens love playing and their
curiosity often finds them
in the most unusual places.

In the countryside, cats often leave their homes shortly before giving birth to find a hidden place where they can give birth to their kittens. In the city, cats find a more or less hidden nook in an apartment or house, and make it comfortable.

Kittens are born deaf and blind and weigh no more than 2 to 4 ounces. Instinctively, they immediately start searching for their mother's teats. For the first few days, kittens wake up only to be fed; sleeping most of the time. Their mothers make special sounds which are intended to keep them huddled by their warm bodies. After ten days, kittens open their eyes for the first time and after three weeks they are able to crawl and clean themselves. As time goes, they become more and more independent and before long they start exploring the world around them.

Cute little kittens

When they get stronger, kittens begin to play and caper about the house, full of energy. All of a sudden they start running backwards and forwards, doing stunts and climbing up brand new curtains. Fortunately, within a few months they become calmer and more placid. Cats are very good at nursing their babies and would even nurse abandoned pups or fox cubs. The cat is a truly excellent mother. It watches its babies most of the time, teaching them all they need to know in order to become adult cats: hygiene, hunting and defence.

A cat is usually prepared to do anything for its kittens. Even though cats hate water, it would certainly jump in if it was necessary to save its offspring. The kittens, on the other hand, take a mischievous pleasure in provoking and teasing the mother. They do all sorts of crazy things to her, which she tolerates with a stoic calm.

At two months, kittens are usually ready to leave the litter, though they still come back. They usually leave for good when they are eight months old. By then, they have reached full maturity and independence.

[1] A cat can have kittens from different fathers in one litter.
[2] This cute little kitten is of the European type.
[3] For the first two weeks, a kitten's eyes are blue.

[4] When a kitten and a mouse grow up together they become friends for life.
[5] Cats love comfort. Their love of fluffy cushions and soft bed covers proves the point.
[6] Kittens can climb trees with ease. Sometimes they have problems getting back down though.

[1] Cats are born after approximately 72 days of gestation.

[2-3] According to the legend, the Sacred cat of Burma originated from a breed which was kept in Burmese temples. This is, however, not entirely true. This breed was in fact created in France in the 1920's by crossbreeding Persian, or Angora, cats with the Siamese breed.

[4] Kittens are not afraid to walk along the tops of very tall structures or along narrow walls. The reason is simple: cats do not suffer from vertigo.

3 [1-3 and right] The Greek islands are full of large and small wild cats which play and sleep on the streets. They are also often fed by the people.

Cats are forever washing themselves. Washing and licking is an obsession.
They should be proud of their reputation as exceptionally clean and tidy animals.

[1-3 and right] The fur of European cat breeds is either monotone, with colors ranging from white, grey, brown, and ginger to coal black, or multicolored. The fur of some cats, though, is a tricolor, usually a combination of black, ginger and white. This coloring is typical for female cats.

Thanks to recent regulations,
this Beauceron pup will not
have its ears clipped.

When they are born, puppies, just like kittens, are blind and deaf and they have no sense of smell. They are very weak and utterly helpless and cannot therefore survive without their mother's care. She usually performs her role impeccably, only leaving her little ones for a few minutes at a time and only when it is absolutely necessary.

She feeds them, licks them carefully in order to keep them clean, and keeps the place tidy by swallowing their excrement. Some time after birth, she shows them the world around them. During the first week, puppies sleep huddled close to one another and wake up every two hours just to eat. After two weeks, they open their eyes and in three weeks' time they can hear and smell. If a puppy strays too far from her, the mother takes it in her mouth by the scruff of its neck and quickly brings it back to where it belongs. After about one month, the puppies start exploring the world around them. When a puppy sees anything moving, it usually reacts in the funniest way.

Puppies from the same litter fight a lot, which is a way of getting to know its four-footed brothers and sisters. The mother often plays an active role in these games, which are a vital part of the dog's education. In this way, puppies try out different real-life situations and thus prepare for their adult life. They learn how to run, hunt, bite and defend themselves. Over the course of these games, a hierarchy is established within the group. The strong dominate the weaker ones, who react by taking up submissive postures: they lie down on their side, with their belly upwards, sometimes letting out a small puddle of wee. At the age of six weeks, a puppy usually knows everything that it needs to become a mature dog. The bitch, having been a devoted and careful mother for the first few weeks, becomes indiffe-

Mischievous puppies

rent as soon as she realises that her puppies can take care of themselves. When the puppies have matured, they neither need, nor miss, their original family. If given the chance, they will mate with members of their family or even with parents or children. Breeders, however, see this behavior as being counter-productive and do not allow it.

[1] Belgian shepherds, or Malinois, always seek the company of their master and his or her whole family, especially the children. [2-3] These cute bulldog puppies are only a few days old and have just opened their eyes.

[4] The Beauceron, or Beauce shepherd, is a great companion; although being such an active and energetic dog, they need a great deal of physical exercise.
[5] The fur of the Jack Russell terrier is mostly white with black or chestnut patches.
[6-7] The King Charles spaniel is a very pleasant, obedient dog, especially good companions for families with young children.

403

[1] Malinois puppies are very active and energetic,
and they just love playing with balls and toys of all sorts.
[2-3] The younger the Shar-Pei, the more wrinkled its skin is.
As it matures, the wrinkles gradually disappear into the
skin, which grows smoother and smoother and in adulthood
is basically free of these deep and distinctive wrinkles.
[4] This small border collie is playing around in the reeds.

[1] Even as an adult, the West Highland white terrier will be a rather small and compact dog.
[2] A young Rottweiler is little more than a cute fluffy ball. If trained badly, an adult can be highly dangerous.
[3] The border collie is a mischievous and playful animal.

In a town, on a farm

[4] The Jack Russell terrier is sometimes referred to as a "rat catcher," as a result of its passion for chasing mice and rats.
[5] In families, Bernese mountain dogs often play the role of cute teddy-bears. These dogs truly love children.
[6] Newfoundlands have actual webs on their feet. Naturally enough, these dogs just love the water.

The owner of these Jack Russell terriers, which are just
a few days old, is carrying them in the pocket of his apron.
In this way, the little puppies will learn to recognize his scent.

These little Canadian huskies are huddling together
to protect themselves against a cold blizzard.

[1-2] The position and shape of the black and chestnut patches on the Jack Russell terrier's head is important in determining their breeding value.

[3] This little St. Bernard puppy will become a huge but very affectionate dog. These dogs are associated with a small keg of rum which St. Bernard dogs used to carry around their necks. This rather practical piece of equipment was meant to help save the lives of mountaineers and climbers in dire straits.

[4] The Jack Russell terrier has become immensely popular with people all over the world, mainly thanks to the film *The Mask*, with Jim Carrey.
[5-7] Siberian huskies grow up in groups. Later in life, they will most probably be harnessed as sled dogs, pulling sleds across vast snowy plains in the freezing north.

One night in spring, a mare gives birth to a foal. She smells her baby and neighs almost inaudibly. As she cleans her baby with her tongue, she leaves her scent on its body - that is the first piece of information the foal stores in its memory. In this way the foal can recognize her in the future. In the early stages of their lives, foals are not able to recognize their mothers other than by their distinctive scent.

With her head, the mare encourages her foal to start moving and stretching its limbs and to stand up on its shaky legs. A foal does not need more than an hour before it can stand up and start suckling from its mother's teats. Only a few days after birth, the foal is already running alongside its mother. It is even able to keep up when she trots, provided that she does not go too fast. The mare cares very well for her foal: she always watches it, keeps it away from curious people, plays with it

and protects it from all danger. Four weeks after birth, foals begin to play together. Friendships are formed which sometimes last for years. Contact with other foals helps them learn to find their place in the group. Young females tend to stay by their mothers more than the males do. At around six months, young horses become independent.

When a newborn donkey comes into the world, the mother tries to pick her baby up by pushing its backside with her head. No more than two days after birth, a baby donkey is up and jumping happily in front of its cautious mother. When it is two months old, it begins to venture further and further from her. And one year after birth, young donkeys leave their mother completely. People say that donkeys are stubborn, indecisive and even dumb. That is however not true at all. Donkeys are in fact intelligent and easy-going animals. As a young animal, a donkey is an ideal play-mate. Donkeys and horses should never be

A foal and a baby donkey

left alone for too long. The everyday presence of people is a necessity. Whether out to pasture or in a stable, these smart and sensitive animals need company. It does not matter whether it is another donkey or a horse. A dog or even a sheep can also be good friends for these large and thoughtful animals.

[1-3-5-6-7] Despite its small and compact body, the Shetland pony is among the strongest of breeds in proportion to its size.

[2] Young foals love trotting alongside their mothers. In this picture we can see a foal and a mare of the Comtois breed.

[4] From a very early age, donkeys feel truly happy outdoors and have a love of difficult terrain.

415

[1] Before a foal can start nibbling and grazing, it must first wait for its molars.

[2] The hair of young ponies is, to a certain extent, curly. As the pony grows older, its hair becomes straight.

[3] A female donkey, or jenny, becomes sexually mature at the age of three or four years.

[4] Shetland ponies feel most at home on the steep, coastal slopes
of the inhospitable Shetland and Orkney Islands in the north of Scotland.

Adult donkeys are very resourceful, hardy animals, and can survive on a very modest diet. They are happy to live off such perennial plants as the thistle.

As Shetland ponies mature, their mane grows longer and thicker.

[1-4] The bond between a donkey foal and its mother is very close, the young animal following its mother everywhere. It is always ready to suckle, and can drink between 5 and 9 pints of milk a day. For a long time, the milk was used as a surrogate for human milk. It is also known to be very beneficial: Queen Cleopatra, the supreme ruler of ancient Egypt, is said to have bathed in donkey's milk.

[5 à 7] Both young and adult donkeys have a gentle, delicate manner of walking. It is not very easy to control them, though, as a result of their often whimsical nature.

These foals have splendid grey hair typical for Arabian horse breeds.

Camargue foals are often born black or dark grey.

There is no better place to have a look at the various kinds of domesticated birds than at a poultry farm. Among others, there are hens, geese and ducks, and the place is full of life and activity. All these rather noisy farm inhabitants wake up at dawn to the call of the rooster, usually as punctual as Swiss clockwork, and they remain active until dusk.

At that time most animals return to their shelters. The commotion and noises of clucking, crowing and cooing fill the air. Turkeys run around, gobbling, while hens get upset and cluck when they are not sat on their eggs of course. Hens lay ten to twenty eggs at a time. Tiny fluffy chicks hatch around twenty one days later. Turkey-hens lay ten to fifteen eggs a year. All these animals take very good care of their young. If they hear a suspicious sound or if they sense danger, they are likely to attack. Geese and ganders defend their nests with great fervour and zeal. They start honking aggres-sively at any intruder. The fox, a predator which often roams around at night, can be deterred simply by adequate fencing.

Every morning, the farmer's wife scatters barley, wheat and corn seeds, which causes even more commotion and excitement among the birds. Now and then, she takes away a few eggs or birds which she uses for her own needs or sells them at the local marketplace. But since the invention of large-scale breeding, poultry has been slowly disappearing from farms. Fortunately, there are still some farms with typical poultry yards. The increasing popularity of eco-farming has led to

A poultry farm

a rediscovery of long-forgotten smells and tastes. Summer holidays on a farm or in a self-catering cottage are once again popular among the urban population, partly because they offer a rare opportunity to see birds and other domesticated animals living in the open air of farmyards, side by side with humans.

[1] The goose usually lays twenty eggs.
[2-3] The hen is an excellent mother: she feeds and protects her chickens with great care.

[4] A female rabbit feeds her babies twice a day.
[5] The bones of Silkie hens are coal black.
[6] During the first six months, chickens change their feathers three times.

[1-2] Goslings are precocial animals; very soon, they are capable of leaving their nest and almost immediately after birth they can run and swim.
[3] A familiar picture: ducklings walking behind their mother. They follow her into the water and immediately start swimming.

[4] Female rabbits usually have 3–7 babies. She keeps the first few hidden away from the world, usually underneath a layer of straw.
[5] At birth, chickens weigh 1.1 ounces and are approximately three inches long.

This lamb, born only a few
hours before the picture was
taken, can already stand on its
weak legs.

After five months gestation, a sheep gives birth to one or two little lambs. Two hours after birth, at the very latest, the newborn animals stand up on their still shaking legs, falter and collapse once or twice, but within moments there they are, walking around happily. Their mother lets them suckle for more than two months, then they start nibbling the grass.

In order to drink, lambs kneel down on their front legs and straddle with their hind legs. They locate the teats, take them in their mouths and, with short abrupt movements, start suckling. For most people it is most impossible to tell one little lamb from another. Their mothers usually succeed in recognizing them by the sound of their bleats. The mother will not allow a lamb to suckle unless she clearly recognizes it by its scent. At this stage, the lamb is still very weak and sometimes it loses contact with its mother, which may result in complete estrangement. If this happens, the bond between mother and infant having been broken, it is up to humans to take care of the abandoned animal and feed it from a bottle until it grows independent.

Sheep live in flocks and do not like to be alone. If a lamb accidentally strays from the flock, it starts bleating and whining out loud until its mother finds it again. As a female lamb grows, it gradually becomes a ewe, a gentle, meek animal. A male, on the other hand, becomes an aggressive ram, unless it is castrated of course. A goat gives birth while standing, the infant landing on straw. This experience is, in a way, somewhat typical for the whole future life of the animal: a cavorting animal always tumbling about. A kid is forever moving and running around. Half an

A gentle lamb, a high-spirited kid

hour after birth, following a few unsuccessful, yet cute and moving, attempts to stand up, the kid finally manages to stand on its legs and in no time you can see it cavorting and jumping around, full of new life.

Thanks to its agility, the goat is most at home in rough, uneven terrain, running up and down steep slopes driven by an inexhaustible energy and joy. First of all, its mother must lick and clean it, absorbing its scent and passing hers on to the newly born animal. Without this, they would not recognise each other later on. Then she feeds her kid with her nutritious milk. After a week, the kid begins to nibble at straw, even while still continuing to suckle. As a fully-grown goat, it will be happy with a quite modest diet: brambles, shrubs or dandelions. It will not hesitate to climb trees to get to young saplings, or will nibble at the bark. Goats are like grass-powered mowers, and sometimes they are let out in particular areas with the intention of allowing them to clear the undergrowth in forests as part of forest fire preventative measures.

Sometimes a mother does not show any interest in her young one. It is then the job of the farmer to take care of the infant himself, instead of its mother. The goat is very protective of her young, especially in the mountains where she has to protect them against eagles, circling in the sky above.

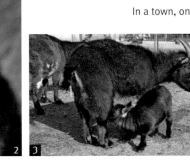

[1-5] Yearlings are born after five months gestation. A goat gives birth to one or two babies. Goats reach sexual maturity at the age of one. A new born yearling weighs approximately 4 pounds and, within a month, she can gain up to 20 pounds. Goats suckle over a period of 4 to 5 months.

[1] Depending on the breed, the fur of the young is either white with black patches or just plain black.
[2] A lamb always stays close to its mother.
[3-4] After birth, lambs need only a very short time before they can stand.

[5] Sometimes lambs mistakenly try to suckle from the wrong sheep.
[6] At the age of 4 to 5 months, most rams are slaughtered for meat.
[7] Some females refuse to suckle their young. In this case, it is necessary to start bottle-feeding them.

At the age of three a lamb is fully grown, though it reaches sexual maturity and is thus capable of reproduction as young as 18 months.

[1-3] Females are kept for breeding as well as dairy produce. The lifespan of a sheep is up to fifteen years.

[4] The wool of some sheep breeds is unusually straight.
[5] Sheep often give birth to twins. Twin lambs usually remain very close throughout their lives.
[6] While playing with its mother, this lamb has climbed on her back.

441

[1] A nanny goat has one or two kids.
[2] Kids just love climbing anything they can.
[3] A kid takes a rest after a long and apparently exhausting feeding.

[4] Lambs' wool can be a variety of colors and hues: from snow white and every imaginable shade of grey, through to chestnut brown or coal black. Many lambs are bicolored.

[1] On goat farms, the kids are fed with powdered milk substitute, and ewe's milk is used instead for the commercial production of cheese and other dairy products.

[3-4] Kids very soon start jumping around on their front and hind legs.

[3] Kids are born after five months gestation.

[5] When out to pasture, kids are forever chewing.
[6] Kids are very agile, climbing very steep slopes and rocks with ease and joy.

445

A cow usually has one calf a year. It is born after nine and a half months gestation.

Acalf is born after nine and a half months gestation. It is almost always an only child as cows only very rarely give birth to more than one calf at a time. The newly-born is covered in hair and born with its eyes open. At birth, a young calf weighs between 66 and 110 pounds and, within several hours of birth, it is capable of taking its first steps –whether out in the fields or in a stable.

During the first few days, a newborn calf spends most of its time either sleeping or feeding on its mother's highly nutritious milk. A cow can only recognise its calf by its scent. The calf confirms by responding to her mooing. The bond between the two is very

A single calf

strong at this time. In order to attract the attention of its mother, and other members of the herd, the calf bleats loudly. This can imply hunger or discomfort.

Later in life, calves become just as calm and apparently contemplative as the adults are. They spend more than eight hours a day grazing. After a calf is weaned, all bonds between mother and calf are broken. A young female must find its place in the herd, while young bulls wait impatiently for mating time.

If a cow happens to lose its calf earlier than normal, she goes through period of intense anxiety, lasting several days. In contrast, once weaned, calves easily cope with the new situation and soon start appreciating the company of other infants in the herd or even of humans.

Calves provide very good quality meat, in particular the so-called milk cattle, which means that calves are kept with their mothers. If a calf is allowed to live, the female becomes a heifer and, after its first litter, is called a dairy-cow. Young steers, or steerlings, are used for reproduction. If they are gelded, when they grow big enough, steers are sold to the slaughterhouse. This is, of course, where all cows eventually end up.

[1] Aubrac cattle from the high-lands of Auvergne in France are among the most persistent and resourceful breed of cattle.
[2] The Limousine breed is highly esteemed for its top quality meat.
[3] Blonde d'Aquitaine cattle are much appreciated by breeders because the animals have a very high fertility rate.
[4] Milking of Saler cattle is a delicate matter, as the presence of the calf is essential for the cows to produce milk.

[5-6] In India, the cow is a sacred animal. This, however, does not prevent them from being kept for milk. The Zebus (*Bos primigenius indicus*) is a typical representative of Indian cattle breeds. [7] A male calf is called a bull and a female, a heifer. An adult, castrated bull is commonly called a steer.

[1-2] Later, these young heifers will be capable of producing more than 1100 pints of milk every month.
[3-4] At first, calves do not leave their mothers' company and neither do they tolerate the presence of another calf.
[5] Only rarely does a cow give birth to a litter of two calves.
[6] Cows that are ready to calve are taken into a cattle-shed; the calf is born on straw.

451

It is not often that assistance is needed at the birth of piglets. Everything usually happens at night. When the time comes, the sow becomes agitated and digs a hole in the ground where, an hour or so afterwards, it gives birth to its piglets. It cleans them thoroughly with its tongue and with its snout pushes them gently towards its many teats.

Each piglet has a teat for itself and if it grabs the wrong one by accident, its owner drives the intruder away. The front teats are richer in milk than the back ones and the piglets therefore compete to get to the front. In order to succeed, piglets can even bite each other quite viciously with their sharp milk teeth. Sows are very fertile and can have four to twelve young in a litter. The record lies with a Danish sow which gave birth to thirty four piglets in a single litter. An hour or so after their arrival into the world, the piglets are trying to stand up on their weak, shaky little legs. It takes only a brief effort and then they are up and running around.

A piglet makes very high-pitched and distinctive grunts. They can be a sign of fear or discomfort. Squealing is used to call others together. When in danger, the sow squeals to warn her young of the danger. If it becomes critical, the sow will not hesitate to attack. When she is digging in the ground with her snout she sometimes happens to grunt as a sign to her piglets that something tasty has turned up. For a long time, piglets have been considered symbols of happiness, mainly because a large litter of piglets had great value for people in the countryside. In China, each

A litter of piglets

year has its own animal symbol; the year of the pig is usually considered lucky. Children born in the year of the pig are said to succeed in all their endeavours. They will be happy both in love and their professional lives and will have a good chance of making their fortune, inheriting or winning a large sum of money.

[1] The suckling pig is a term used for an unweaned piglet, one which is still being fed by its mother. They are usually under 6 months old.

[2] A sow is very attentive to her young and is likely to become aggressive if anyone gets too close to them.

[3] The European sow has twelve teats on her belly.

[4-5-6] Pigs which grow up outdoors usually produce better quality meat. Unlike pigs from large-scale breeding farms, they rarely suffer from disease.

[1] Piglets just love rolling in mud. It is a very effective way of getting rid of parasites.

[2-4] The Chinese pig is an umbrella term for all pig breeds with typically black hair.

[3] Contrary to popular belief, pigs are not filthy animals. If they live outdoors, pigs and their offspring are clean and pink.

[1-2] A mud bath always means playtime for young piglets.

[3] Piglets are born after 114 days gestation.

[4] Sometimes there are piglets of different colors in one litter.

[5] It has been more than 5000 years since people domesticated pigs.

[6] Pigs often move from one place to another, organised into families in which both the males and females watch over their young.

Index

This index provides
a list of animals shown
in the photographs.

461

PHOTOGRAPHY CREDITS
All the photographs in this book are the property of Horizon Features